CONTENTS

1. Summary of Findings 06

2. Audience Profile 12

3. Visitors to London 36

4. Theatre Visits 44

5. Visit Satisfaction 56

6. Booking Tickets 64

7. Booking Fees 80

8. Ticketing Services 92

9. Factors Influencing Frequency 96

10. Motivations for Visit 102

11. Marketing and Communication 110

12. Media Consumption 120

13. Internet Usage 130

14. Expenditure 140

15. Travel to Theatre 150

16. Access 156

17. Appendices 159

1 SUMMARY OF FINDINGS

Photographer: Carl O'Connell

AUDIENCE PROFILE

Women make up the majority of theatregoers (68%), as was the case in 2003 and 1997. 2008 saw a small but continuing increase in the proportion of female visitors. The average age of adult theatregoers is 43.

Seven in ten theatregoers work either full or part time, a small but significant increase from 2003. The average income of theatregoers is £31,500. Male theatregoers and those from overseas earn more than average. As in 2003, theatregoers of white ethnic origin represent by some way the largest grouping.

Only a small proportion of theatregoers come to the theatre on their own. The size of the average party is 3.3 individuals, a considerable fall from 2003. The most common party size is two people and in line with this, just under half of theatregoers are visiting with their partner; three in ten visit with friends and a quarter with other family members.

RESIDENCE AND VISITING LONDON

Four in five theatregoers are from the UK; 2008 saw a substantial decline in the proportion of overseas visitors, with a particular fall in the proportion of North American visitors. Amongst UK visitors there has been a shift away from theatregoers resident in the South East with a greater proportion of theatregoers coming from other parts of the UK.

On average, those who do not live or work in London stay 7.3 nights, but three in ten are visiting for a day trip only. The average is clearly influenced by longer stays of overseas visitors as very few UK based visitors stay more than 4 nights.

Amongst those visiting London, the majority go to the theatre only once during their stay and this group has grown since 2003. Just under half of this group describe visiting the theatre as the main reason they came to London.

The average number of theatre trips that theatregoers have made in London in the last 12 months is 6.4, which mirrors results from 2003. The average number of visits to the theatre outside London is a little lower at 4.6. Musicals remain the most commonly attended performance; seven in ten have been to a musical in London in the last 12 months, as was the case in 2003 and 1997.

Other than visiting the theatre, almost three quarters of theatregoers have been to the cinema in the last 12 months; this has increased since 2003. Similarly, two thirds of theatregoers have been to a museum or gallery in the last 12 months.

La Cage aux Folles

SATISFACTION WITH VISITING THE THEATRE

Three in five theatregoers rate their overall enjoyment of their visit to the theatre as very good; this has climbed since 2003. When asked about the performance itself, three quarters describe it as very good; again, this is above the level seen in 2003.

Half of theatregoers rate their ticket as good value for money. Theatre staff are well rated and these levels have increased compared to 2003 and 1997. As in previous years, the comfort of the seating and the toilets caused the highest levels of dissatisfaction.

BOOKING TICKETS

The methods for booking theatre tickets have seen some noticeable shifts since 2003, especially with increased use of the internet.

Two thirds book their ticket within one month of the performance, with one in five (19%) booking on the day of the performance. This has fallen from 2003 when more than a quarter of bookings (27%) were made on the day. Generally, 2008 has seen a slight shift towards tickets being booked further in advance of the performance.

There has been a clear and marked increase in the number of theatregoers booking their tickets over the internet, increasing from 17% in 2003 to 48% in 2008. Correspondingly there have been decreases in the proportion of theatregoers booking in person and particularly over the telephone. Amongst those booking online, using the internet at home is the most common response.

The sources from which tickets were booked are also considerably influenced by the rise of the internet. Three in ten book through a website – 16% through a show or theatre website and 15% through another website – both almost double the proportions seen in 2003. This compares with 1997 when just 1% of theatregoers booked online. Purchasing directly from the theatre box office whether by phone or in person has seen a considerable decrease, from around half of theatregoers previously booking in this way to a third now. In addition, there is limited use of fan-to-fan or auction sites when booking tickets currently.

Just under half of theatregoers bought their ticket at full price and two in five bought it at a discounted rate. This is a slight increase from 2003 when just over half paid full price for their tickets.

Having to pay full price for their ticket would have put a third of theatregoers off visiting the theatre. Encouragingly just over one in five would have come anyway.

BOOKING FEES

The impact of and attitudes towards booking fees on theatre tickets was explored in our online survey. Theatregoers have a fairly limited understanding of why booking fees and transaction fees are charged. A majority of theatregoers do not feel that booking fees are currently at the right level. Theatregoers report paying on average £2.69 in booking fees. Unsurprisingly, they view the level as too high and think that this charge should be £1.30. Just over half would like to see the cost of booking fees incorporated into the price of tickets.

When looking at the relationship between booking fees and ticket buying, half agree that the presence of a booking fee does impact on their ticket buying behaviour and just over half agree that the size of the booking fee impacts on ticket buying. Responses indicate that the presence of any booking fee at all impacts on ticket buying as much as the level of the fee.

Transaction fees were also unpopular, with the great majority feeling that a transaction fee should not be charged when a booking fee is also levied.

A small proportion of theatregoers (24%) are aware that a restoration levy is also charged on tickets for some theatres. In contrast to the feelings around booking fees mentioned above, theatregoers are not entirely opposed to the idea of paying a contribution to the restoration of theatres in the West End. On average theatregoers would be happy to pay over £1 per ticket towards these funds.

The attraction of certain new ticketing services was also explored in the online survey. The most popular potential service was being able to print off your own theatre tickets at home or work to then be scanned at the theatre. The service with the least support was the option to pay via your mobile phone bill when booking on a ticketing website.

VISITING THE THEATRE

The overwhelming majority of theatregoers visit the theatre to be entertained. Other key factors which encourage people to visit the theatre include the show's reputation, a personal recommendation, a special offer or promotion and positive reviews in the media.

A number of different aspects can influence people to see a particular show. The top aspects which influenced people to visit the theatre in 2008 are in line with 2003, namely; the show's reputation generally, a personal recommendation, good reviews in the media and a price or special promotion.

Furthermore, various different sources of information encourage theatregoers to visit the theatre. Word of mouth is the stand-out source of information that is effective in encouraging people to go to the theatre, mentioned by two-thirds of theatregoers. Other key sources of information are the press, mentioned by almost half of theatregoers, what's on listings, websites and advertising posters, all mentioned by over three in ten theatregoers.

In addition, by far the main way in which theatregoers find out or hear about a production is via word of mouth, mentioned by half of all theatregoers. This is followed by the press, websites, what's on listings, advertising posters and the fact that some had seen the production before.

It is also worth noting that two in five theatregoers (who completed the online survey) regularly watched one of the recent theatre-based reality TV programmes, increasing to over half of those attending a musical. Three in ten said they had watched 'Any Dream Will Do' and/or 'How Do You Solve A Problem Like Maria', while a quarter had watched 'I'd Do Anything'. Almost half of those who had watched such a show, said it made them more likely to attend the featured musical, while a third said it encouraged them to attend a musical generally.

On the other hand, the perception that visiting the theatre is expensive is the key reason which puts theatregoers off visiting the theatre more often, followed by not having enough time. When looking at visiting the theatre in London specifically, as well as issues around price, a number of other key factors are around transport - namely problems with parking, public transport finishing too early, safety on public transport and the congestion charge.

Positively, seven in ten theatregoers strongly agree that West End Theatre makes up an important part of London's culture, while over half of theatregoers strongly agree that theatres make the West End a vibrant place and that they are vitally important to London's tourism. Furthermore, a quarter of theatregoers strongly agree that visiting West End theatre is an important part of their life, while a further third tend to agree that it is.

EXPENDITURE

As would be expected, people are spending more money visiting the theatre now than ever before, generating significant income for the London economy.

The average amount spent going to the theatre is now £118 (among all theatregoers) an increase of £31 over the last five years. It is worth noting, however, that overseas visitors spend on average £174 and UK residents living outside London spend £160, while London residents only spend on average £69. This no doubt reflects the additional costs incurred by overseas and non-London residents such as travel and accommodation. It is also perhaps more of a special occasion going to London and visiting the theatre for non-London residents and this is likely reflected in the amount of money spent as a result of their visit.

The main costs associated with going to the theatre (among all theatregoers) are tickets (£40), transport to and from London (£24), accommodation (£22), and eating out (£20), with each element increasing significantly over the past five years - £31, £16, £15 and £16 respectively.

Carousel

2 AUDIENCE PROFILE

GENDER

Female visitors account for more than two thirds of theatregoers (68%); males make up just 32%. This compares to 65% and 35% respectively in 2003 and 61% and 39% in 1997.

- It is suggested that women are more likely to complete questionnaires, introducing some bias towards females in the results, but this would have affected the previous years of the survey as well. 2008 has seen a slight, but continuing increase in the proportion of female visitors.

- Amongst younger visitors, the proportion of females is even greater (73% of those aged under 34 are female and 27% are male). This also applies to UK visitors coming from outside London (71% female and 29% male).

- Women are also more likely to be visiting in a larger or organised group, with 81% of those in an organised group being women.

- Those seeing a musical are more likely to be women (71%), whereas men are more likely to be seeing a play (38%) or an opera (47%).

Gender

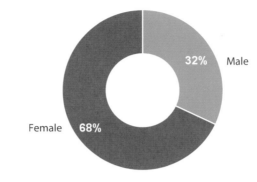

Gender	2008 (%)	2003 (%)	1997 (%)
Male	32	35	39
Female	68	65	61

Base: All answering (2008: 4160, 2003: 6357, 1997: 6880)

Source: Ipsos MORI

ARE YOU......?

	Gender %		Age %				Origin %			*Performance Type %				Income %			Working Status %	
	M	F	16-24	25-34	35-54	55+	London	Rest of UK	Overseas	M	P	O	D	Up to £20,000	£20,001 - £50,000	£50,001+	Working	Not Working
Base	1440	2720	537	797	1379	1337	1721	1644	717	2089	935	763	318	1255	1562	746	2776	1300
Male	100	-	27	27	32	40	33	29	36	29	38	47	26	21	34	54	33	30
Female	-	100	73	73	68	60	67	71	64	71	62	53	74	79	66	46	67	70

*Performance Type key:
M = Musical
P = Play
O = Opera
D = Dance
NB: Entertainment type performances are not reported here due to the small base size

AGE

The age spread of theatregoers is fairly even, and has changed little since 1997. The average age of all theatregoers aged 15 and above has remained consistent at 43. It is important to note that, for practical reasons, those aged under 15 are not included in this research. The actual average age of theatregoers, including those aged under 15, would be lower than 43.[1]

- Overseas visitors have the youngest age profile (23% are aged 16-24 and the average age is 42), as do visitors from London for whom the average age is 41.

- Visitors of non-white ethnic origin are likely to be younger with one quarter under the age of 24 (24%) and a further third aged between 25 and 34 (32%). This might indicate an attitudinal shift with younger visitors of non-white ethnic origin being more disposed to visiting the theatre than older generations. It could also reflect the diversity of shows now on offer in the West End.

Age

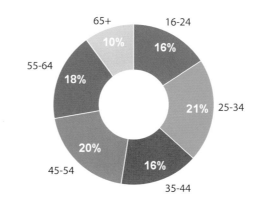

Base: All answering (2008: 4098, 2003: 6242, 1997: 6880)

Age	2008 (%)	2003 (%)	1997 (%)
16-24	16	16	13
25-34	21	20	21
35-44	16	18	20
45-54	20	18	23
55-64	18	19	15
65 and over	10	10	8

Source: Ipsos MORI

Younger visitors also represent a greater proportion of those who buy their ticket on the day of the performance (24% of 16-24 year olds) and have a ticket that is free (29% amongst 16-24 year olds). This might reflect the lifestyle of younger visitors who display more impulsive buying habits and are less likely to plan theatre visits well in advance than their older counterparts.

- The average age of a theatregoer attending an opera performance is 56, with 61% of those attending aged 55 and over. This compares to an average age of 42 amongst those seeing a musical.

---

1 Only those aged 15+ are included in the survey as interviewing children is subject to strict rules and guidelines which require parental consent to be gained before the child is interviewed. This is not practical given the methodology of this project and as such those aged under 15 were not included in the research. It is likely that, if those aged under 15 were included, the average age of theatregoers would be considerably younger.

HOW OLD ARE YOU?

THE WEST END THEATRE AUDIENCE   15

	Gender %		Age %				Origin %			*Performance Type %				Income %			Working Status %	
	M	F	16-24	25-34	35-54	55+	London	Rest of UK	Overseas	M	P	O	D	Up to £20,000	£20,001 - £50,000	£50,001+	Working	Not Working
Base	1409	2641	547	805	1394	1352	1698	1614	710	2055	927	745	317	1252	1555	743	2743	1273
16-24	13	17	100	-			15	12	23	18	12	3	11	31	6	3	10	29
25-34	18	23		100			31	15	17	21	21	10	26	16	31	14	27	8
35-44	16	16			44		16	17	14	17	15	9	14	11	19	21	20	6
45-54	20	20			56		15	25	19	22	18	17	17	14	20	30	25	9
55-64	20	17				65	15	20	19	16	22	32	19	16	15	24	16	23
65 or over	14	7				35	9	11	8	7	12	29	13	11	8	8	3	26
Average age	45.74	41.44	20.48	28.96	45.27	63.32	40.54	45.56	41.51	41.54	45.22	55.64	43.92	40.08	42.76	47.70	41.27	46.66

*Performance Type key:
M = Musical
P = Play
O = Opera
D = Dance
NB: Entertainment type performances are not reported here due to the small base size

ETHNICITY

Visitors giving their ethnicity as 'white' are by far the largest group - 92% of theatregoers are of white ethnic origin. Amongst those of non-white ethnic origin, no single group dominates. This matches the profile of visitors seen in 2003. As in the previous section visitors of non-white ethnic origin tend to be younger than those of white ethnic origin.

- Thirteen per cent of theatregoers from London are from a non-white ethnic background. This is higher than for all UK based visitors, where those of non-white ethnic origin represent 7% of audience members. Although the survey cannot claim to be representative of the national population and we have to take into account those who did not complete the questionnaire, the proportion of visitors from an ethnic minority is similar to that of the population as a whole (7.9% in the 2001 census, although some now consider this to be a conservative figure[2]).

- As one would expect, the nature of the show also appears to impact on the profile of visitors, with 'Hip-Hop' inspired musical 'Into the Hoods' attracting a larger proportion of black or black British visitors than other shows (17%).

Ethnicity

	White	92%
Asian/Asian British	2%
Mixed	2%
Other	2%
Chinese	1%
Black/Black British	1%

	2008 (%)	2003 (%)
White	92	92
Non-White	8	8

Base: All answering (2008: 4122, 2003: 6365)

Source: Ipsos MORI

2   Data from 2001 Census – please see national statistics website: http://www.statistics.gov.uk/cci/nugget.asp?id=455

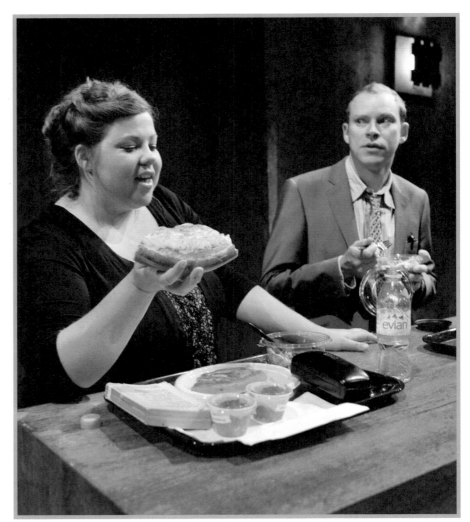

Fat Pig

WHAT IS YOUR ETHNIC ORIGIN?

	Gender %		Age %				Origin %			*Performance Type %				Income %			Working Status %	
	M	F	16-24	25-34	35-54	55+	London	Rest of UK	Overseas	M	P	O	D	Up to £20,000	£20,001 - £50,000	£50,001+	Working	Not Working
Base	1406	2666	541	800	1361	1326	1700	1636	709	2078	930	746	315	1258	1552	748	2757	1286
White	93	92	87	88	93	96	87	97	89	92	92	96	91	92	93	93	92	91
Asian or Asian British	3	2	2	5	2	1	4	1	4	3	2	1	2	2	2	3	2	3
Mixed	1	2	3	2	2	*	3	1	1	2	1	1	3	2	1	1	2	1
Other	1	2	3	2	1	1	2	*	3	1	2	1	2	2	1	1	1	3
Chinese	1	1	3	2	1	1	2	*	3	1	1	1	2	1	1	1	1	1
Black or Black British	1	1	2	1	1	*	2	*	1	1	1	*	1	1	2	*	1	1
Non-white	7	8	13	12	7	4	13	3	11	8	8	4	9	8	7	7	8	9

*Performance Type key:
M = Musical
P = Play
O = Opera
D = Dance
NB: Entertainment type performances are not reported here due to the small base size

WORKING STATUS

Seven in ten theatregoers work either full- or part- time. Amongst those not working, retirees and students make up the largest group.

The proportion of theatregoers working full-time is directly in line with 2003 (at 55%) but the proportion working part-time increased to 16% (from 12% in 2003).

- London-based visitors see the highest proportion of full-time workers at 62% (compared to just 49% of overseas visitors).

- In terms of the type of performance, retired visitors are prevalent at opera performances (38%), reflecting the older age profile that this genre attracts. Musicals attract the largest proportion of theatregoers who are working (72%).

Working status

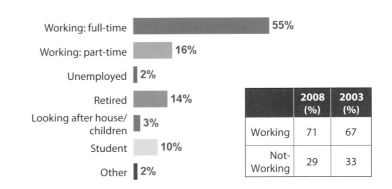

Working: full-time	55%
Working: part-time	16%
Unemployed	2%
Retired	14%
Looking after house/children	3%
Student	10%
Other	2%

	2008 (%)	2003 (%)
Working	71	67
Not-Working	29	33

Base: All answering (2008: 4126, 2003: 6371)

Source: Ipsos MORI

Blood Brothers

WHICH BEST DESCRIBES YOUR WORK STATUS?

	Gender %		Age %				Origin %			*Performance Type %				Income %			Working Status %	
	M	F	16-24	25-34	35-54	55+	London	Rest of UK	Overseas	M	P	O	D	Up to £20,000	£20,001 - £50,000	£50,001+	Working	Not Working
Base	1416	2660	530	793	1364	1329	1706	1632	711	2064	934	757	318	1265	1554	751	2809	1317
Working – full time	66	50	31	83	69	30	62	52	49	56	54	39	56	29	77	72	78	
Working – part time	7	20	13	6	19	19	14	20	11	16	14	15	16	27	9	9	22	
Unemployed	2	1	1	2	1	1	2	1	1	1	2	1	3	2	1	1		5
Retired	17	12	*	*	2	47	11	16	13	11	17	38	15	16	10	11		47
Looking after house/children	*	4	*	3	6	1	2	3	4	3	3	2	3	2	1	4		10
Student	7	11	53	5	1	1	8	6	19	10	9	4	6	22	1	1		33
Other	2	2	1	1	2	2	1	1	3	2	2	1	1	2	1	1		5
Working	72	70	45	89	88	48	75	72	60	72	68	54	71	56	86	81	100	
Not working	28	30	55	11	12	52	25	28	40	28	32	46	29	44	14	19		100

*Performance Type key:
M = Musical
P = Play
O = Opera
D = Dance
NB: Entertainment type performances are not reported here due to the small base size

A Midsummer Night's Dream. Photographer: Manuel Harlan

ANNUAL INCOME

The average annual income of theatregoers in 2008 is £31,500 (based on those prepared to disclose their income). Amongst overseas visitors this increases to £36,120. Male theatregoers earn on average £39,900; this is substantially higher than female visitors.

- As may be expected, average income increases with age, but those aged 35-54 earn the most (£37,640 on average).

- In the UK, London residents have the highest income at £33,600. Amongst overseas visitors, North American visitors earn the most (£38,000).

- Opera and plays are the genres that attract the highest earners with the average income of a member of these audiences earning £38,800 and £38,000 respectively.

Average annual income

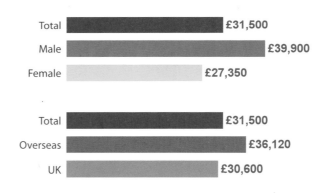

Total	£31,500
Male	£39,900
Female	£27,350
Total	£31,500
Overseas	£36,120
UK	£30,600

Base: All answering (2008: 3613, 2003: 4648)

Source: Ipsos MORI

PLEASE INDICATE YOUR APPROXIMATE ANNUAL INCOME IN £ STERLING

	Gender %		Age %				Origin %			*Performance Type %				Income %			Working Status %	
	M	F	16-24	25-34	35-54	55+	London	Rest of UK	Overseas	M	P	O	D	Up to £20,000	£20,001-£50,000	£50,001+	Working	Not Working
Base	1275	2288	447	725	1229	1149	1532	1438	580	1787	827	681	276	1277	1578	758	2536	1034
Up to £10,000	10	23	58	8	12	16	15	21	24	21	14	10	16	51			10	44
£10,001-£20,000	13	21	20	18	14	23	17	22	11	19	14	21	14	49			18	20
£20,001-£35,000	28	30	17	43	28	25	32	30	20	30	25	21	37		65		33	15
£35,001-£50,000	19	14	2	19	20	15	18	13	17	15	18	17	15		35		18	8
£50,001-£75,000	13	6	*	8	12	9	9	7	12	7	12	14	8			46	10	5
£75,001+	17	6	3	4	14	13	11	7	16	8	16	17	9			54	10	9
Up to £20,000	23	44	78	26	26	39	31	43	35	40	28	31	31	100			28	63
£20,001-£50,000	46	44	19	62	48	40	49	43	36	45	44	38	52		100		52	23
£50,001+	30	13	3	12	26	22	20	14	29	15	28	31	17			100	20	14
Average income (000s)	39.88	27.25	14.11	30.89	37.64	33.13	33.58	27.94	36.12	29.18	38.01	38.83	31.91	9.90	32.73	71.88	34.63	22.55

*Performance Type key:
M = Musical
P = Play
O = Opera
D = Dance
NB: Entertainment type performances are not reported here due to the small base size

WHO ARE YOU VISITING WITH?

Forty-five percent of theatregoers are visiting with a partner, the most frequently mentioned person to visit with. Three in ten (31%) visitors are attending with friends. Only 6% of audience members are visiting the theatre alone.

This breakdown is similar to that seen in 2003, where a partner was again the most common person to be visiting with (44%).

The number of theatregoers visiting as part of an organised group has dropped considerably since 1997 and 2003 (16% and 14% respectively) to just one in twenty (5%) in 2008. However, this may be attributed to questionnaire design, as the 1997 and 2003 questionnaires asked in a separate question if they were attending in an organised group.

- There are small but significant increases in the proportions of people who visit with children under 16 and with other family members.

- These shifts in the proportion of family groups are mirrored by falls in the number of people visiting with friends and work colleagues.

- Those attending alone are more likely to be men (9%), overseas visitors (10%), of non-white ethnic origin (9%) and visiting an opera (20%), dance performance (11%) or a play (10%).

Who are you visiting the theatre with today?

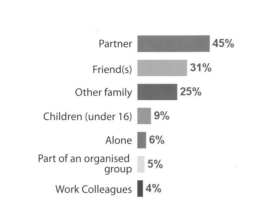

	2008 (%)	2003 (%)
Partner	45	44
Friend(s)	31	35
Other family	25	21
Children (under 16)	9	7
Alone	6	7
Part of an organised group	5	14
Work Colleagues	4	8

Base: All answering (2008: 4141, 2003: 6391)

Source: Ipsos MORI

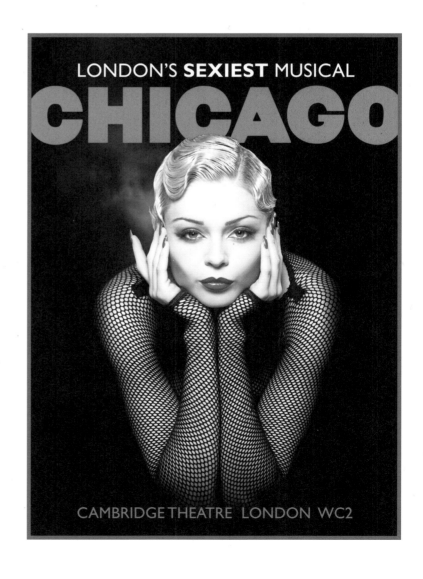

WHO ARE YOU VISITING THE THEATRE WITH TODAY?

	Gender %		Age %				Origin %			*Performance Type %				Income %			Working Status %	
	M	F	16-24	25-34	35-54	55+	London	Rest of UK	Overseas	M	P	O	D	Up to £20,000	£20,001-£50,000	£50,001+	Working	Not Working
Base	*1390*	*2619*	*527*	*771*	*1344*	*1309*	*1716*	*1640*	*709*	*2070*	*935*	*761*	*323*	*1245*	*1521*	*729*	*2699*	*1280*
Partner	64	36	25	43	47	54	42	48	43	43	51	46	38	35	46	61	46	40
Friend(s)	22	35	38	38	27	26	40	25	28	31	30	30	30	32	31	24	31	32
Other family	17	29	33	21	26	23	21	28	26	28	19	12	23	29	23	22	25	26
Children (under 16)	7	9	4	4	18	3	5	12	11	12	3	1	5	8	8	11	10	5
Alone	9	5	4	6	6	7	6	5	10	4	10	20	11	6	6	7	6	7
Part of an organised group	3	5	10	1	4	5	3	5	6	5	4	2	3	6	2	5	3	8
Work colleagues	3	4	4	4	4	3	3	5	2	4	2	2	4	3	4	4	5	1
Other	*	*	*	-	*	-	*	*	*	*	*	*	-	*	-	*	*	*
With others	94	95	96	94	94	93	94	95	90	96	90	80	89	94	94	93	94	93

*Performance Type key:
M = Musical
P = Play
O = Opera
D = Dance
NB: Entertainment type performances are not reported here due to the small base size

PARTY SIZE

The average size of party is 3.3 people; this is a drop from 2003 when the average party size was 6.3 and more in line with 1997 where the average group contained 3.6 people.

This question was asked slightly differently in 2008[3], which may influence this change, but the proportions of people visiting in a group of 8 or more people is substantially smaller than in 2003, but consistent with 1997.

- The most common group size is two (57%) which corresponds to the large number of people visiting with their partner (45%).

- Women are likely to visit in a slightly larger group (7% as part of an organised group), potentially reflecting their likelihood to visit with friends.

- North American visitors visit in the largest groups (4.2 people on average) potentially reflecting the popularity of organised tours amongst these visitors.

- On average, there are 4 people in a party when tickets are booked more than a month in advance, showing the influence of organised trips.

Including yourself, how many people are there in your personal party attending the performance today?

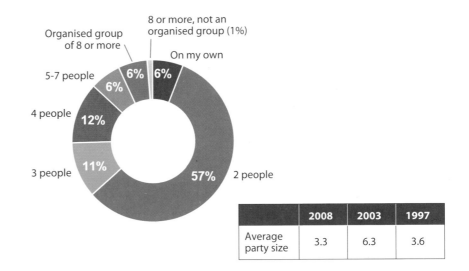

	2008	2003	1997
Average party size	3.3	6.3	3.6

Base: All answering (2008: 4135, 2003: 6075, 1997: 6680)

Source: Ipsos MORI

- Musicals attract the largest average party size of any genre (3.5 people) compared to just 2.3 for those attending the opera. Coach party visits are an important component of musicals audiences.

---

3   In 2008 those who came in groups of 8 or more people were asked to specify whether the group had made an organised group booking or not. In 2003 respondents were simply asked about the number of people in their group and not whether a group booking had been made. The 2008 figure is therefore more likely to be an accurate indicator of party size as defined by 'single organised ticket purchase'.

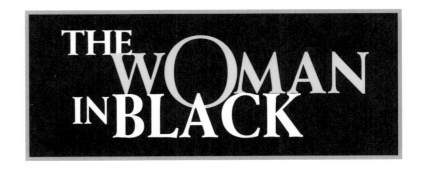

INCLUDING YOURSELF, HOW MANY PEOPLE ARE THERE IN YOUR PERSONAL PARTY ATTENDING THE PERFORMANCE TODAY?

	Gender %		Age %				Origin %			*Performance Type %				Income %			Working Status %	
	M	F	16-24	25-34	35-54	55+	London	Rest of UK	Overseas	M	P	O	D	Up to £20,000	£20,001 - £50,000	£50,001+	Working	Not Working
Base	1391	2619	523	772	1349	1305	1707	1642	709	2061	935	761	326	1239	1526	728	2711	1274
On my own	9	5	4	6	7	7	6	5	10	4	10	20	11	6	7	7	6	8
2 people	59	57	58	63	52	60	61	57	48	55	60	61	63	57	60	55	58	56
3 people	8	12	12	11	12	8	11	9	14	11	9	9	11	11	10	11	11	9
4 people	12	12	8	10	15	11	11	12	14	14	10	6	8	11	12	13	12	12
5-7 people	7	6	7	6	8	4	6	7	7	8	4	2	3	6	7	7	7	5
Part of an organised group of 8 or more (group booking made)	4	7	10	3	6	7	3	8	6	7	5	2	3	8	4	5	5	8
Part of an organised group of 8 or more (NO group booking made)	1	1	1	1	1	2	1	1	1	1	1	*	1	1	1	2	1	1

*Performance Type key:
M = Musical
P = Play
O = Opera
D = Dance
NB: Entertainment type performances are not reported here due to the small base size

GENRE

Musicals made up the greatest proportion of performances seen by theatregoers in 2008[4]. More than two in three theatregoers saw a musical (66%). One in five audience members were attending a play (21%). Those seeing opera, dance and performance/ entertainment performances make up smaller proportions – dance 6%, opera 4% and performance/entertainment 3%. This profile has changed only a little since 2003.

Women (68%), those in the youngest age group (16-24, 74%); theatregoers from elsewhere in the UK (77%) and Europe (78%) are more likely than average to see a musical (66% of all theatregoers are seeing a musical).

- Those attending the theatre in a larger group (75% of those visiting as part of an organised group and 76% of those visiting with 5 or more people) and those whose ticket was reduced or discounted are more likely to see a musical (71%).

- Those who visit the theatre less often are also more likely to see a musical (74% of those who are making their only theatre visit in the last 12 months and 71% of those who have visited between 2 and 5 times in the last 12 months).

Theatregoers seeing a play are more likely than average (on average 21% of theatregoers are seeing a play) to be male (25%), aged over 55 (26%), living in London (29%) or from North America (39%).

Genre

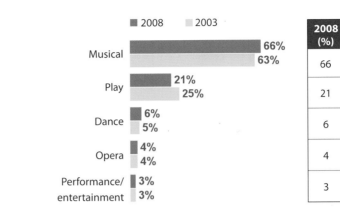

	2008 (%)	2003 (%)
Musical	66	63
Play	21	25
Dance	6	5
Opera	4	4
Performance/entertainment	3	3

Base: All answering (2008: 4586, 2003: 6716)

Source: Ipsos MORI

- Those visiting the theatre alone are more likely to see a play (33%).

- Theatregoers seeing a play are also more likely to visit the theatre most frequently (28% of those making 6 or more visits to the theatre in the last 12 months).

- Those earning the most are more likely to be attending a play (33%).

Six per cent of theatregoers are attending a dance performance. This is higher amongst certain groups - women (7%) aged either 25-34 (9%) or over 55 (8%) and London residents (11%).

- Those attending alone (13%) or with one other person (8%) are more likely to be attending a dance performance.

- Those earning between £20,001 and £50,000 are more likely to be attending a dance performance (8%).

Theatregoers attending an opera performance have a similar profile to those attending a dance production in a number of ways – they are also more likely to be over 55 (10%), to be London residents (7%), to be visiting alone (14%) or with one other person (5%).

- However, they are also more likely to be men (6%), of white ethnic origin (5%), not working (7%) and earning over £50, 000 (8%).

- Younger theatregoers (4% aged 16-24 and 5% aged 25-34), an overseas resident (6%), those who book their ticket on the day of the performance (5%) and those earning less than £20,000 (4%) are more likely than average to be seeing a performance/entertainment (3% of all theatregoers).

---

4   This is representative of London West End theatre as a whole as the data has been weighted based on box office sales data provided by SOLT.

Gender can play a large part in determining the choice of performance. As such a detailed breakdown of the attendance at different genres by male and female visitors is set out below.

	Musical (%)	Play (%)	Opera (%)	Dance (%)
Male	29	38	47	26
Female	71	62	53	74

August: Osage County. Photographer: Michael Brosilow

PERFORMANCE TYPE

	Gender %		Age %				Origin %			*Performance Type %				Income %			Working Status %	
	M	F	16-24	25-34	35-54	55+	London	Rest of UK	Overseas	M	P	O	D	Up to £20,000	£20,001 - £50,000	£50,001+	Working	Not Working
Base	1440	2720	547	805	1394	1352	1876	1773	824	2333	1060	797	336	1277	1578	758	2809	1317
Musical	60	68	74	64	70	55	52	77	64	100	-	-	-	70	66	52	67	62
Play	25	19	16	20	19	26	29	13	25	-	100	-	-	16	21	33	20	23
Opera	6	3	1	2	3	10	7	3	1	-	-	100	-	4	4	8	3	7
Dance	6	7	5	9	6	8	11	5	3	-	-	-	100	6	8	6	7	7

*Performance Type key:
M = Musical
P = Play
O = Opera
D = Dance
NB: Entertainment type performances are not reported here due to the small base size

Boris Godunov. Photographer: Clive Barda

WHERE DO AUDIENCE MEMBERS LIVE?

Four in five audience members are from the UK (80%) and amongst these nearly half (38%) are from London.

The proportion of UK based visitors has increased since 2003 when 73% of theatregoers were from the UK. The 2008 results are closer to the figure seen in 1997 when 82% of audience members were UK residents.

Twenty percent of audience members are from overseas, with European visitors and those from North America making up the largest groups. In line with the increase observed for UK based visitors, the proportion of overseas visitors has fallen compared to 2003 and is more closely aligned with the profile seen in 1997 where 18% of audience members were from overseas.

Compared to 2003, the group that has seen the largest fall is North American visitors (17% in 2003 down to 7% in 2008). It is likely that the strength of the pound in 2008, which made visiting the UK expensive for American tourists, has affected these figures.

It is worth noting that these figures relate to West End theatre as a whole across the second half of 2008. It is likely that a musical in the summer tourist season could attract a greater proportion of overseas visitors than this figure.

The London boroughs of Camden and Wandsworth see the highest proportions of visitors (both 7%), followed by Lambeth, Southwark and Westminster (all 6%) (figures are based on all those giving a valid London postcode).

Where do you live?

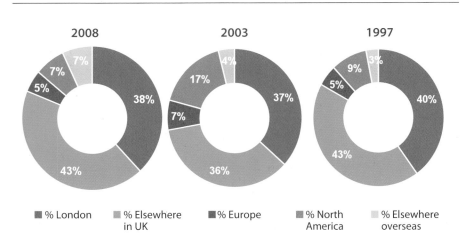

2008   2003   1997

■ % London   ■ % Elsewhere in UK   ■ % Europe   ■ % North America   % Elsewhere overseas

Note: On this chart the key reads left to right
Base: All answering (2008: 4473, 2003: 6612, 1997:6880)

Source: Ipsos MORI

This spread across London closely reflects that which we saw in 2003. Although the overall proportion of London residents is higher in 2008, we have not seen this increase concentrated in any particular boroughs, rather small shifts across a number of them.

WHERE DO YOU LIVE? LONDON

London Borough	2008 (%)	2003(%)	1997(%)
Wandsworth	7	6	6
Camden	7	6	8
City of Westminster	6	6	7
Lambeth	6	5	5
Southwark	6	5	4
Barnet	5	5	5
Lewisham	4	3	2
Islington	4	4	4
Ealing	4	4	3
Richmond upon Thames	4	4	4
Bromley	4	4	3
Haringey	4	4	4
Kensington and Chelsea	3	5	6
Hammersmith & Fulham	3	4	4
Brent	3	3	3
Enfield	3	2	3
Merton	3	3	2
Tower Hamlets	2	3	1
Hackney	2	2	2
Kingston upon Thames	2	1	2
Greenwich	2	2	2
Waltham Forest	2	3	2
Harrow	2	2	2
Hounslow	2	2	2
Redbridge	2	2	1
Croydon	2	2	4
Sutton	1	2	1
Hillingdon	1	2	2
Bexley	1	2	1
Havering	1	1	2
Newham	1	1	1
City of London	0	1	1
Barking & Dagenham	0	*	1

Base: All London residents giving a valid postcode (2008: 1,260, 2003: 2,616)

WHERE DO YOU LIVE? UK OUTSIDE LONDON

Outside London, three in five (60%) theatregoers are from the South East. One in ten UK residents living outside London are from the Midlands, the North and the South West. Smaller proportions come from the home nations – Scotland (4%), Wales (3%) and Northern Ireland (1%). Areas which are within easy commuting distance of the West End have the greatest proportions of theatregoers – Kent and Surrey lead the way – both with 9%.

The profile of visitors from outside London is similar to 2003, but there has been a significant fall in the proportion

of visitors coming from the South East and a corresponding increase in the proportion of visitors coming from the rest of the UK (other than the South East) compared to the proportions seen in both 2003 and 1997.

Area	2008 (%)	2003 (%)	1997 (%)
South East	60	69	71
Midlands	11	9	7
North	11	9	11
South West	10	8	5
Scotland	4	3	2
Wales	3	2	3
Northern Ireland	1	0	1

Base: All UK residents living outside London and giving a valid UK postcode (2008: 1,404, 2003: 1,731,1997: 4,272)

WHERE DO YOU LIVE? OVERSEAS

Top mentions only

A number of English-speaking countries make up the largest proportions of overseas visitors. Twenty nine per cent of overseas visitors are from the United States, 10% from Australia, 8% from Canada and 5% from Ireland.

- Looking at this compared to 2003 and 1997, and bearing in mind the overall drop in overseas visitors, the proportion of visitors from the United States has fallen (29% of overseas visitors in 2008 compared to 45% in 2003 and 1997), but there has been an increase in visitors from Australia (10% of overseas visitors compared to 3% and 7% respectively), Canada (8% compared to 4% and 7%) and Ireland (5% compared to 1% in both previous years).

Region	2008 (%)	2003 (%)	1997 (%)
USA	29	45	45
Australia	10	3	7
Canada	8	4	7
Ireland	5	1	1
Denmark	3	*	-
New Zealand	3	1	2
Netherlands	2	2	3
Norway	2	2	1
Germany	2	3	7
France	2	1	2
Sweden	2	2	5
Spain	2	1	*
Italy	2	1	1
South Africa	2	1	2
Other	27	30	13

Base: All overseas visitors (2008: 824, 2003:1,840, 1997: 1,764)

WHERE DO YOU LIVE?

THE WEST END THEATRE AUDIENCE

	Gender %		Age %				Origin %			*Performance Type %				Income %			Working Status %	
	M	F	16-24	25-34	35-54	55+	London	Rest of UK	Overseas	M	P	O	D	Up to £20,000	£20,001 - £50,000	£50,001+	Working	Not Working
Base	1377	2622	522	785	1341	1296	1876	1773	824	2216	1007	778	327	1239	1539	730	2714	1254
London	40	38	38	55	33	33	100	-	-	31	52	61	63	33	44	42	41	33
Rest of UK	41	46	34	31	51	50	-	100	-	51	26	35	30	51	43	33	45	43
Europe	6	5	9	7	5	3	-	-	26	7	3	1	3	5	5	6	5	6
North America	8	7	13	3	6	8	-	-	37	6	14	2	2	6	5	13	5	11
Other overseas	5	4	5	4	4	5	-	-	37	5	5	1	2	4	4	5	4	6

*Performance Type key:
M = Musical
P = Play
O = Opera
D = Dance
NB: Entertainment type performances are not reported here due to the small base size

3 VISITORS TO LONDON

STAYING IN LONDON

Amongst those who do not live or work in London, 32% of all visitors (i.e. from the rest of the UK and overseas) are visiting London for a day trip only. This is almost exactly in line with 2003 when 31% of visitors were visiting the capital only for a day.

For those who do stay overnight the average number of nights stayed in the capital is 7.3 nights or roughly a week.

Amongst UK theatregoers from outside London, just under half (48%) are visiting for the day only. Amongst those who are staying overnight, 1 night is the most common period to stay for (18%), with very few UK based visitors staying more than 4 nights. The average number of nights per stay is 3.1.

This compares to 2003, where 58% of domestic visitors were on a day trip to London and the average number of nights stayed was 2.6.

Amongst overseas visitors, the average number of nights stayed in London is 11.5, a small increase from 2003. As might be expected, European visitors stay for the shortest period on average (5.4 nights) whilst visitors from North America stay the longest (18.1 nights). This mirrors patterns seen in 2003, but the average number of nights American visitors are staying in London has increased since both 2003 and 1997 (from 11.8 in 2003 and 10.3 in 1997). The number of nights European visitors are staying is similar to 2003 but a little lower than in 1997.

- Younger visitors tend to be spending a longer period of time in London (15.5 nights for those aged 16-24). This group are more likely to be travelling, taking a gap year or studying in London.

On this visit to London, how many nights will you be staying?

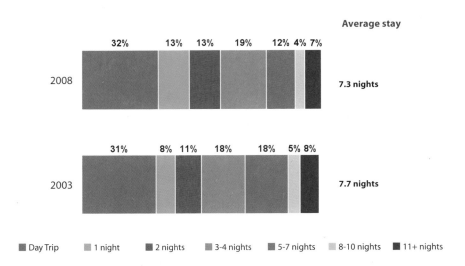

Note: On this chart the key reads left to right
Base: All answering who do not live or work in London (2008: 2226, 2003: 3542)

Source: Ipsos MORI

On this visit to London, how many nights will you be staying?

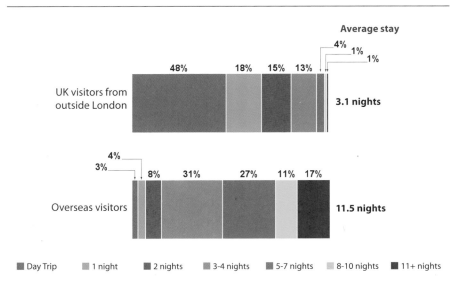

Note: On this chart the key reads left to right
Base: All answering who do not live or work in London (UK visitors from outside London: 1431, Overseas visitors: 795)

Source: Ipsos MORI

- Those who are not working stay on average a greater number of nights in London (10.9). This most likely reflects the greater amount of leisure time available, e.g. retirees.

- Those visiting the theatre as part of a larger party (and potentially also visiting London as part of a group, although we do not know for certain) are likely to be staying in London for longer. 18.1 nights is the average stay for those visiting the theatre in parties of 5 of more and 28.0 nights for those visiting the theatre as part of an organised group.

- Audience members who are seeing a play have a longer average stay in London (13.6 nights on average) particularly compared to those seeing musicals (5.8 nights on average).

ON THIS VISIT TO LONDON, HOW MANY NIGHTS WILL YOU BE STAYING?

	Gender %		Age %				Origin %			*Performance Type %				Income %			Working Status %	
	M	F	16-24	25-34	35-54	55+	London	Rest of UK	Overseas	M	P	O	D	Up to £20,000	£20,001 - £50,000	£50,001+	Working	Not Working
Base	669	1338	299	272	741	694	-	1431	795	1378	442	266	97	692	712	338	1314	702
Day trip only	32	36	26	33	36	31		48	3	34	22	54	46	38	35	22	35	28
At least one night	68	65	74	67	64	69		52	97	66	78	46	54	62	62	78	65	72
1	13	14	13	16	13	13	-	18	4	14	8	11	16	13	13	12	13	12
2	13	12	11	12	13	13	-	16	8	14	9	8	6	14	14	12	13	13
3-4	19	17	19	18	19	20	-	13	31	19	19	10	10	17	17	18	20	19
5-7	12	11	12	11	11	13	-	4	27	11	18	10	13	9	9	20	11	13
8-10	4	4	4	5	4	4	-	1	11	4	8	2	2	2	2	9	4	5
11-14	2	1	1	3	2	2	-	*	4	1	8	1	3	1	1	3	2	1
15+	6	5	13	3	3	3	-	1	13	3	12	3	4	7	7	3	2	9

Base: All answering who do not live or work in London

*Performance Type key:
M = Musical
P = Play
O = Opera
D = Dance
NB: Entertainment type performances are not reported here due to the small base size

NUMBER OF THEATRE VISITS WHILST IN LONDON

A third of visitors (33%) who do not live or work in London will visit the theatre more than once while they are staying in the capital. However, the majority of visitors (67%) will make only one visit.

The average number of visits to the theatre whilst staying in London is 2.3. Since 2003 there has been an increase in the proportion of visitors making only one theatre visit whilst in London (67% vs. 57%).

- The average number of visits has fallen from 2.45 to 2.26 representing the greater proportion of visitors making only one visit to the theatre whilst staying in London in 2008. This average is still higher than that seen 10 years ago in 1997 when it stood at 2.18.

- Younger visitors make a higher than average number of visits to the theatre. Those aged 16-24 make on average 3.5 visits whilst staying in London.

- Overseas visitors make a higher number of theatre visits whilst staying in London – the average is 3.8

- Amongst overseas visitors, those from North America make the greatest number of visits – on average 5.4.

- Theatregoers at plays are likely to be making a larger number of theatre visits while in London – 3.7 compared to 2.0 for those at musicals and 1.8 at opera and 1.9 at dance.

During this visit to London, how many times (including this performance) will you go to the theatre?

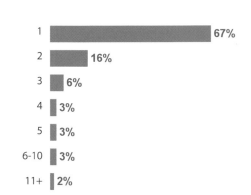

	2008 (%)	2003 (%)	1997 (%)
1	67	57	62
2	16	20	15
3	6	9	9
4	3	5	
5	3	2	
6-10	3	4	
11+	2	3	

Base: All answering who do not live or work in London (2008: 2163, 2003: 3601, 1997: 3542)   Source: Ipsos MORI

- Those attending the theatre alone make a great number of visits while staying in London – on average 3.1.

- The highest levels are seen amongst those visiting as part of an organised group – these visitors make on average 3.6 visits to the theatre.

- It seems that many of these visits are not planned in advance as those buying tickets on the day of the performance also have a higher than average number of visits (2.7).

The Phantom Of The Opera

DURING THIS VISIT TO LONDON, HOW MANY TIMES (INCLUDING THIS PERFORMANCE) WILL YOU GO TO THE THEATRE?

	Gender %		Age %				Origin %			*Performance Type %				Income %			Working Status %	
	M	F	16-24	25-34	35-54	55+	London	Rest of UK	Overseas	M	P	O	D	Up to £20,000	£20,001 - £50,000	£50,001+	Working	Not Working
Base	674	1304	290	258	723	679	-	1424	739	1337	435	258	96	687	697	321	1270	689
1	65	68	60	75	70	64	-	80	41	69	51	77	75	69	72	59	70	62
2	15	16	15	13	15	19	-	12	24	16	18	10	12	14	16	18	15	17
3	7	6	7	5	7	5	-	4	12	6	8	6	3	6	4	8	6	7
4	3	3	1	1	3	4	-	2	5	2	5	1	2	3	2	4	3	3
5	3	2	2	3	2	4	-	1	6	2	4	1	3	2	3	5	2	3
6-10	3	2	5	2	2	2	-	1	6	2	6	4	3	2	2	2	2	4
11+	3	2	8	1	1	2	-	1	6	1	7	*	2	4	1	3	1	4
More than once	35	32	40	25	30	36	-	20	59	31	49	23	26	31	28	41	30	38
Mean score	2.65	2.10	3.46	1.81	1.91	2.33	-	1.49	3.80	1.99	3.74	1.80	1.90	2.46	1.84	3.00	2.09	2.66

Base: All answering who do not live or work in London

*Performance Type key:

M = Musical

P = Play

O = Opera

D = Dance

NB: Entertainment type performances are not reported here due to the small base size

HOW IMPORTANT IS A THEATRE TRIP IN MAKING A DECISION TO VISIT LONDON?

Going to the theatre is the main reason for a trip to London for just under half (47%) of non-London based theatregoers. For a further third (33%), a theatre trip is fairly important. Thus, a total of 80% of theatregoers from outside London cited their theatre visiting as an important factor in choosing to visit the capital. At the other end of the spectrum, 20% of theatregoers rated it not very (12%) or not at all (8%) important.

- Predictably, given their location and easier access to information, UK residents (from outside London) are especially likely to say that visiting the theatre is the main reason for their visit to London (65%).

- Those visiting the theatre in larger parties are more likely to mention the theatre as the main reason for visiting London (61% of those in a group of 5 or more and 64% of those visiting in an organised party). This also applies to those who booked their ticket more than a month ago (68%) suggesting that there are organised groups of theatregoers making plans to visit London mainly for a theatre visit.

- A visit to the theatre is more likely to be the main reason for visiting London for those seeing an opera or dance performance (68% and 65% respectively compared to just 33% for those seeing a play).

Overall, how important was your theatre trip in persuading you to visit London?

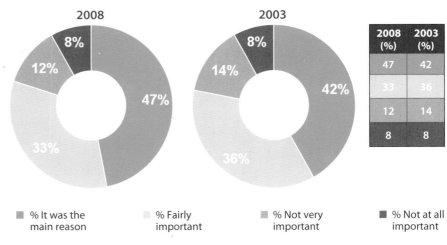

	2008 (%)	2003 (%)
% It was the main reason	47	42
% Fairly important	33	36
% Not very important	12	14
% Not at all important	8	8

■ % It was the main reason   ■ % Fairly important   ■ % Not very important   ■ % Not at all important

Base: All answering who do not live or work in London (2008: 2293, 2003: 3724)   Source: Ipsos MORI

- Amongst overseas theatregoers, 13% cite theatre as the main reason for their visit to London, with 49% deeming it fairly important – a total of 62% for whom theatregoing is a positive factor. In 2003, the corresponding figures were 14% (main reason) and 54% (fairly important). London theatre thus remains a significant factor for overseas visitors planning a trip, but it presumably takes its place alongside such factors as London's heritage and tourist attractions as well as its place as a travel hub for visiting elsewhere in the UK.

OVERALL, HOW IMPORTANT WAS YOUR THEATRE TRIP IN PERSUADING YOU TO VISIT LONDON?

	Gender %		Age %				Origin %			*Performance Type %				Income %			Working Status %	
	M	F	16-24	25-34	35-54	55+	London	Rest of UK	Overseas	M	P	O	D	Up to £20,000	£20,001 - £50,000	£50,001+	Working	Not Working
Base	*711*	*1379*	*300*	*275*	*752*	*731*	-	*1490*	*803*	*1423*	*454*	*273*	*101*	*717*	*727*	*341*	*1334*	*737*
It was the main reason	43	50	44	46	50	56	-	65	13	49	33	68	65	53	49	34	49	44
Fairly important	33	33	29	25	34	38	-	25	49	32	42	21	26	31	33	40	32	36
Not very important	13	11	18	16	9	10	-	6	24	12	15	6	6	11	11	11	11	13
Not at all important	11	6	9	13	7	6	-	4	15	7	11	6	3	5	7	15	8	7
Important	76	83	73	71	84	85	-	90	62	81	74	86	91	83	82	74	81	80
Not important	**24**	**17**	**27**	**29**	**16**	**15**	**-**	**10**	**38**	**19**	**26**	**11**	**9**	**17**	**18**	**26**	**19**	**20**
Mean score	3.08	3.27	3.08	3.04	3.27	3.25	-	3.50	2.60	3.24	2.97	3.51	3.53	3.31	3.24	2.96	3.22	3.17

Base: All answering who do not live or work in London

*Performance Type key:
M = Musical
P = Play
O = Opera
D = Dance
NB: Entertainment type performances are not reported here due to the small base size

4 THEATRE VISITS

HOW OFTEN DO YOU VISIT THE THEATRE IN LONDON?

Four in five (80%) audience members have been to the theatre in London more than once in the last 12 months. Just under half (47%) have been to the theatre more than 3 times in the last twelve months. Overall, the average number of visits is 6.4 which indicates that many theatregoers are committed attenders of West End theatre.

The most dedicated visitors are the 5% of audience members who have been to the theatre 21 or more times over the last 12 months – this represents seeing one performance every two and a half weeks, more in some cases.

At the other end of the scale, one in five visitors (20%) are making their only visit to the theatre in the last 12 months.

Whilst we would expect London-based visitors to be the most frequent visitors (on average 8.8 visits in the last 12 months), overseas visitors make on average 4.3 visits a year and those from elsewhere in the UK 4.9 visits. Attending the theatre is obviously a key part of trips to London for some audience members.

- Those attending the theatre alone have made 13.8 visits on average in the last 12 months. Those visiting with at least one other person make only 6 trips to the theatre each year.

- As would be expected, those with a higher annual income make more visits to the theatre in London on average than those with a lower annual income. For those earning up to £20,000 the average number of visits is 6.6 compared to 7.6 for those earning £50,001+.

Including this performance, how many times have you been to a London theatre during the last 12 months?

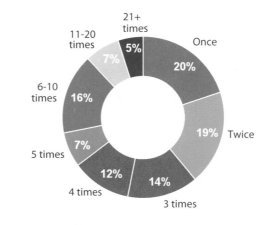

Base: All answering (2008: 3944, 2003: 5934)

Source: Ipsos MORI

	2008	2003
Average number of visits	6.4	6.2

- Those attending an opera performance have made on average 14 visits in the past twelve months. This is perhaps explained by the type of theatregoer who attends this type of performance (older, higher income, etc). While those attending a musical have visited the theatre on average only 4.9 times in the last twelve months.

Grease

INCLUDING THIS PERFORMANCE, HOW MANY TIMES HAVE YOU BEEN TO A LONDON THEATRE DURING THE LAST 12 MONTHS?

	Gender %		Age %				Origin %			*Performance Type %				Income %			Working Status %	
	M	F	16-24	25-34	35-54	55+	London	Rest of UK	Overseas	M	P	O	D	Up to £20,000	£20,001 - £50,000	£50,001+	Working	Not Working
Base	1253	2382	463	705	1227	1191	1769	1524	584	1910	928	760	307	1110	1389	669	2448	1156
1	19	19	23	20	21	16	8	21	42	23	14	5	42	21	17	18	20	19
2	17	20	21	19	21	17	14	25	17	23	12	8	20	20	21	13	19	18
3	13	15	11	17	15	13	14	16	11	16	13	9	11	13	15	13	14	13
4	12	12	10	12	13	11	12	13	7	12	11	8	16	11	12	12	12	10
5	7	7	6	7	6	8	9	6	4	7	7	6	-	6	7	9	7	7
6-10	17	16	17	15	16	18	23	11	11	13	22	26	11	16	16	19	16	17
11-20	9	7	8	6	6	10	12	4	5	4	14	21	-	7	7	11	7	9
21+	7	4	4	5	4	7	8	3	3	3	7	18	-	6	5	6	5	7
More than once	81	81	77	80	79	84	92	79	58	77	85	95	58	79	83	82	80	81
More than 3 times	51	45	45	45	44	55	64	38	29	39	51	79	27	46	47	56	47	50
More than 5 times	33	27	29	27	25	35	43	19	18	20	43	64	11	28	28	39	28	33
Mean score	7.68	5.79	5.84	6.08	5.45	8.05	8.83	4.91	4.27	4.91	8.36	13.99	2.55	6.63	6.08	7.56	6.06	7.44

*Performance Type key:

M = Musical
P = Play
O = Opera
D = Dance

NB: Entertainment type performances are not reported here due to the small base size

VISITS TO THE THEATRE OUTSIDE LONDON

A third (37%) of London audience members have also been to the theatre outside London more than once in the last 12 months. Again, there appears to be a committed band of theatregoers with one in ten visitors having been to the theatre outside London on more than five occasions.

Overall, the average number of visits to non-London theatres is 4.6 visits per 12 months.

One in six audience members have been to the theatre outside London just once in the last 12 months and one in eight have made two visits. It is worth noting that almost half (47%) of theatregoers have not been to the theatre outside London in the last 12 months.

The question was asked somewhat differently in 2003, when the theatre outside London was included as part of a list of other leisure activities therefore we cannot make direct comparisons in terms of the number of visits. But 37% of theatregoers in 2003 stated they had been to the theatre outside London in the last 12 months, this compares to 53% who have been to the theatre outside London in the last 12 months in 2008.

- Overseas visitors visit theatres outside London more often than the average – 6.6 visits a year.

How many times have you been to the theatre in the UK outside London during the last 12 months?

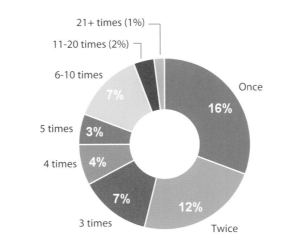

21+ times (1%)
11-20 times (2%)
6-10 times
7%
5 times 3%
4 times 4%
3 times 7%
Once 16%
Twice 12%

Base: All answering: (4251)

Source: Ipsos MORI

Visits outside of London	2008
Average	4.6

Dirty Dancing

HOW MANY TIMES HAVE YOU BEEN TO A THEATRE IN THE UK, OUTSIDE LONDON DURING THE LAST 12 MONTHS?

	Gender %		Age %				Origin %			*Performance Type %				Income %			Working Status %	
	M	F	16-24	25-34	35-54	55+	London	Rest of UK	Overseas	M	P	O	D	Up to £20,000	£20,001 - £50,000	£50,001+	Working	Not Working
Base	747	1408	274	318	723	809	806	1208	711	1161	490	499	144	718	808	372	1398	742
1	28	30	31	42	31	20	37	25	11	30	27	22	33	29	32	28	31	26
2	22	24	23	18	26	24	25	24	6	24	26	18	20	22	24	25	25	21
3	12	12	12	11	11	14	10	14	4	12	12	13	18	12	13	10	11	14
4	8	8	7	5	9	10	7	10	2	9	7	9	6	10	6	7	7	10
5	6	7	5	7	6	6	5	8	2	6	6	8	5	7	6	8	7	7
6-10	16	12	11	11	11	18	11	13	7	13	13	20	12	12	13	16	12	15
11-20	6	4	6	4	4	5	4	4	2	4	6	7	4	5	4	4	4	5
21+	3	2	4	2	3	2	2	2	2	2	3	3	2	3	3	2	2	3
More than once	72	70	69	58	69	80	63	75	25	70	73	78	67	71	68	72	69	74
More than 3 times	38	34	34	29	33	42	29	37	15	35	35	47	39	37	31	38	33	39
More than 5 times	24	19	21	17	17	25	18	19	11	19	22	30	18	20	19	22	19	23
Mean score	5.10	4.50	5.73	4.09	4.40	4.79	4.24	4.31	6.60	4.35	5.48	5.61	4.24	4.99	4.31	4.98	4.51	5.06

*Performance Type key:

M = Musical

P = Play

O = Opera

D = Dance

NB: Entertainment type performances are not reported here due to the small base size

PERFORMANCE TYPES SEEN OVER THE LAST YEAR

Musicals remain the most commonly attended type of performance in the last twelve months. Seven in ten (70%) theatregoers have attended a musical, which is in line with 2003 when 67% attended a musical.

Forty two per cent have attended a play in the last twelve months, 34% a comedy, 29% a dance performance, while 19% have been to an opera. In addition, 12% of theatregoers have been to an entertainment performance in the last twelve months.

• Female theatregoers are more likely to have been to a musical in the past year - 73% of females compared to 64% of men.

• Male theatregoers are more likely than women to have been to a play, comedy or opera within the last 12 months.

• Younger audiences (16-34) are more likely to have seen a comedy in the last year (38% for both 16-24 and 25-34 year olds), whereas older theatregoers (55+) are more likely to have been to a play, dance or opera.

• Theatregoers from London are more likely to attend a broad variety of performance genres. Three quarters (75%) have been to a musical, three in five (60%) to a play and around half (48%) to a comedy. This is consistent with the greater ease of attendance for Londoners.

• Overseas visitors however, have been to see a more confined genre range. A third (35%) of those from Europe and 28% of those from North America have not been to another type of performance in the last year.

Which, if any, of the following types of performance have you been to in London during the last 12 months?

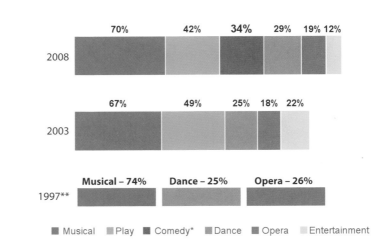

Note: On this chart the key reads left to right
Base: All answering (2008: 4251, 2003: 6577, 1997: 6880)
* Comedy was not included on the questionnaire in 2003
** Question was asked differently in 1997, the chart shows those performances which are directly comparable

Source: Ipsos MORI

WHICH, IF ANY, OF THE FOLLOWING TYPES OF PERFORMANCE HAVE YOU BEEN TO IN LONDON DURING THE LAST 12 MONTHS?

THE WEST END THEATRE AUDIENCE

49

	Gender %		Age %				Origin %			*Performance Type %				Income %			Working Status %	
	M	F	16-24	25-34	35-54	55+	London	Rest of UK	Overseas	M	P	O	D	Up to £20,000	£20,001 - £50,000	£50,001+	Working	Not Working
Base	1360	2570	521	766	1303	1278	1821	1656	698	2109	987	779	326	1207	1500	716	2647	1254
Musical	64	73	71	71	73	66	75	72	54	77	59	47	59	73	71	64	71	69
Play	46	41	41	41	39	50	61	30	30	29	79	69	49	37	44	54	41	46
Comedy	39	32	38	38	31	32	48	25	27	30	52	29	27	30	36	45	35	30
Dance	28	30	29	28	28	33	41	24	17	25	29	40	67	29	31	29	30	28
Opera	24	17	12	14	17	31	30	13	9	10	26	90	41	17	20	28	18	23
Entertainment (e.g. circus, cabaret etc)	11	12	16	14	11	8	19	8	6	11	15	11	9	11	12	12	12	10
Other	11	9	8	10	9	12	13	8	7	8	11	19	14	9	10	11	10	10
None	12	11	15	11	11	11	2	12	31	14	9	2	5	12	10	10	11	13
Any	88	89	85	89	89	89	98	88	69	86	91	98	95	88	90	90	89	88

*Performance Type key:

M = Musical

P = Play

O = Opera

D = Dance

NB: Entertainment type performances are not reported here due to the small base size

LEISURE ACTIVITIES OTHER THAN THE THEATRE

Theatregoers have undertaken a range of cultural activities in the UK other than attending the theatre in the last 12 months. Cinema heads the list: almost three quarters of theatregoers (73%) have been to a cinema in the last 12 months. In addition, a large proportion of audience members (66%) have visited a museum or art gallery in the last year (this is significantly greater than for the UK population as a whole where 42% have visited a museum or gallery in the last 12 months)[5]. Theatregoers obviously also enjoy museums and galleries.

This mirrors the results in 2003 where these two activities were again the most popular. However, the proportion of audience members going to the cinema has increased from 67%, while visiting a museum or gallery remains largely in line (68%).

Two in five (41%) theatregoers have been to a visitor attraction (such as Madame Tussauds) in the last year. This is exactly the same proportion as was seen in 2003. Live music concerts remain popular with theatregoers – 37% have attended a classical or jazz concert and 34% a pop/rock/hip-hop concert. Both of these proportions have increased since 2003, from 28% and 29% respectively.

Three in ten (30%) audience members have been to a dance club and similar proportions have attended a live sporting event (28%). Theme parks (20%) and stand-up comedy (18%) are a little less popular, but both have again seen a small increase compared

to 2003 (theme parks from 16% and stand-up comedy from 14%).

Overall, one in twenty theatregoers (5%) have not undertaken any of these other activities at all within the last 12 months; this stays consistent with 2003 where 6% of theatregoers undertook no other activities.

The popularity of other leisure activities has remained remarkably consistent between 2003 and 2008, suggesting that theatregoers' interests have remained constant across the last 5 years and the rationale for cross-marketing different cultural activities – particularly the theatre, cinema and museums/galleries - remains just as valid.

- Women are more likely to have been to the cinema in the last year (75%), as are those aged 25-34 (82%) and those who are working (76%).

- Theatregoers aged over 55 are more likely to have visited a museum or art gallery (71%), as are London residents (79%) and those not working (71%). This is likely to be linked to the proportion of retired people in the over 55 age group.

- Those aged 16-24 are more likely than average to have been to a visitor attraction (55%) as are overseas visitors (56%). This is the only activity which overseas visitors are more likely to have done, reflecting the fact that they are visiting the UK as tourists.

- Men (41%) are more likely to have been to a classical or jazz concert as are those aged over 55 (45%), white theatregoers (38%) and those earning over £50,000 (41%).

Other than London theatre, please tick any of these things that you have visited/attended in the UK, in the last 12 months ?

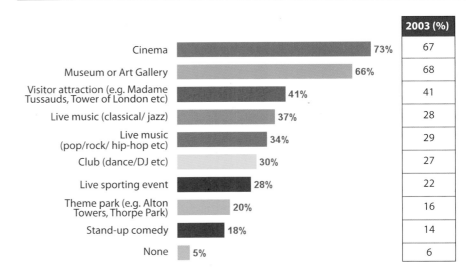

	2003 (%)
Cinema 73%	67
Museum or Art Gallery 66%	68
Visitor attraction (e.g. Madame Tussauds, Tower of London etc) 41%	41
Live music (classical/ jazz) 37%	28
Live music (pop/rock/ hip-hop etc) 34%	29
Club (dance/DJ etc) 30%	27
Live sporting event 28%	22
Theme park (e.g. Alton Towers, Thorpe Park) 20%	16
Stand-up comedy 18%	14
None 5%	6

Base: All UK residents answering (2008: 4180, 2003: 6511)   Source: Ipsos MORI

5   Taking Part Survey, 2006-2007 Annual data: http://www.culture.gov.uk/images/research/TP-surveyAnnualData-0607.pdf

- Women are more likely to have been to a rock/pop/hip-hop concert (36%) along with younger theatregoers (45% of 16-24 year olds and 48% of 25-34 year olds) and those who are working (39%).

- As would be anticipated younger theatregoers are more likely to have been to a dance club (68% of 16-24 year olds) as are non-white theatregoers (40%). We have seen previously that non-white theatregoers tend to be younger so this is likely to influence this.

- Those earning under £20,000 are more likely to have been to a dance club – again this reflects the younger audience as income tends to increase with age.

- Live sport events attract more male visitors (37%) and those earning more than £50,000 (36%).

- Both theme parks and stand-up comedy attract more younger theatregoers (35% and 27% respectively amongst 16-24 year olds).

Stomp

OTHER THAN LONDON THEATRE, PLEASE TICK ANY OF THESE THINGS THAT YOU HAVE VISITED/ATTENDED IN THE UK, IN THE LAST 12 MONTHS?

	Gender %		Age %				Origin %			*Performance Type %				Income %			Working Status %	
	M	F	16-24	25-34	35-54	55+	London	Rest of UK	Overseas	M	P	O	D	Up to £20,000	£20,001 - £50,000	£50,001+	Working	Not Working
Base	1374	2600	522	771	1337	1288	1755	1675	673	2090	953	766	321	1239	1530	725	2692	1253
Cinema	69	75	76	82	72	66	88	82	25	73	75	75	79	74	76	69	76	68
Museum or Art Gallery	68	66	65	67	63	71	79	55	67	58	82	88	81	63	68	74	65	71
Visitor attraction (e.g. Madame Tussauds, Tower of London)	39	41	55	42	40	32	39	36	56	44	34	27	39	40	41	40	41	41
Live music (classical, jazz)	41	36	33	37	35	45	47	38	15	30	48	67	54	35	41	41	37	39
Live music (pop/rock/hip-hop etc)	32	36	45	48	35	18	42	38	10	36	36	15	30	33	39	33	39	23
Club (dance/DJ)	29	30	68	53	18	6	41	26	16	31	29	12	29	36	30	22	31	26
Live sporting event	37	24	28	29	30	25	33	31	9	28	30	24	27	23	31	36	30	24
Theme park (e.g. Alton Towers, Thorpe Park)	17	21	35	23	21	7	18	27	7	24	13	5	11	24	19	13	21	16
Stand-up comedy	18	18	27	31	14	7	24	18	5	17	23	10	16	19	21	17	20	13
None	5	4	5	2	5	6	2	2	17	6	3	1	3	5	4	5	4	6
At least one	94	96	95	98	95	94	98	98	83	94	97	99	97	95	96	95	96	94
Live music	56	56	56	61	54	53	67	58	22	50	63	71	67	53	60	57	58	51

*Performance Type key:
M = Musical
P = Play
O = Opera
D = Dance
NB: Entertainment type performances are not reported here due to the small base size

5 VISIT SATISFACTION

SATISFACTION WITH VISITING THE THEATRE

Overall, satisfaction with visiting the theatre in the West End remains high. Of those theatregoers giving an opinion[6], 63% rate their overall enjoyment of their visit as 'very good' – representing a slight increase on 2003 (61%).

The highest levels of satisfaction are seen for the performance itself, with three quarters of theatregoers rating the performance as very good (75%), slightly above the level in 2003 (70%).

Half (51%) of theatregoers rate their ticket as very good value for money. This is in line with results seen in 2003 (48%), and is particularly striking, given the increase in average ticket prices between 2003 and 2008.

Theatre staff are well rated by audience members and 2008 has seen their ratings increase even further. Just under half (48%) rate them as very good, compared to 41% in 2003 and 37% in 1997.

However, different aspects of the theatregoing experience score less well.

The comfort of the seating receives the highest level of negative rating - 14% rate the comfort of the seating as poor, 10% rate the toilets as poor, while 8% of audience members rate the overall comfort of the auditorium as poor. This is in line with the results seen in 2003, and represents a continuing challenge for many theatres.

On the flip side, an increased proportion of theatregoers rate toilets as very good (19% in 2003 versus 24% presently).

Both the box office and the foyer/lobby of theatres receive respectable 'very good' ratings (45% and 35% respectively). Consistent with previous years, the lowest positive ratings are for catering and refreshments (other than bars) (13%), but this is likely to be influenced by many audience members not having used these specific services.

How would you rate each of the following at this theatre today?

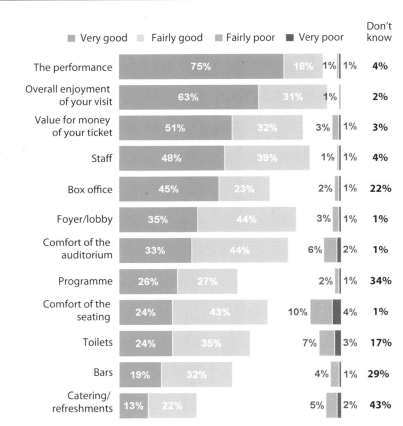

Base: All answering each question (3285 – 3897)   Source: Ipsos MORI

How would you rate each of the following at this theatre today? – Top 6 changes over time

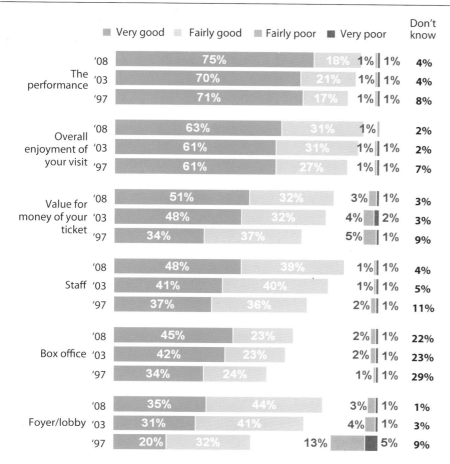

Base: All answering each question (2008: 3285 – 3897, 2003: 5223 – 6049, 1997: 6880)   Source: Ipsos MORI

How would you rate each of the following at this theatre today? – Bottom 6 changes over time

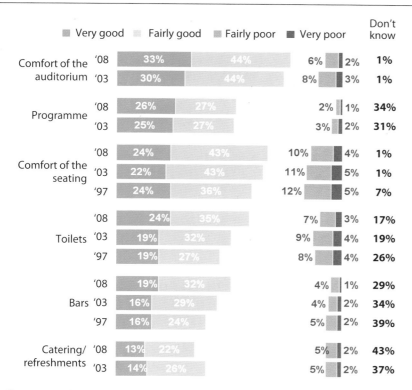

Base: All answering each question (2008: 3285 – 3897, 2003: 5223 – 6049, 1997: 6880)   Source: Ipsos MORI

Chicago The Musical

OVERALL ENJOYMENT OF VISIT

- Women (66%), those aged 35-54 (66%), those living in the UK (particularly those from outside London – 66%), white theatregoers (63%), those who booked their ticket at least a month in advance (67%) and those earning less than £20,000 (66%) are more likely to rate their overall enjoyment of their visit as very good. The dance genre has the highest overall enjoyment rating (71% very good).

- Many of these groups who are positive about their overall enjoyment are also likely to rate the performance as very good. Those who are particularly likely to rate the performance positively are audience members from elsewhere in the UK (79%), those booking their ticket at least a month in advance (79%) and those seeing a musical (78%).

- Those who rated their overall enjoyment as poor are also more likely to rate the toilets and comfort of seating as poor (24% for toilets and 34% for comfort of seating), suggesting that these can be issues fundamental to overall enjoyment.

HOW WOULD YOU RATE EACH OF THE FOLLOWING AT THIS THEATRE TODAY?

	Gender %		Age %				Origin %			*Performance Type %				Income %			Working Status %	
	M	F	16-24	25-34	35-54	55+	London	Rest of UK	Overseas	M	P	O	D	Up to £20,000	£20,001 - £50,000	£50,001+	Working	Not Working
Base	1284	2396	502	738	1254	1134	1572	1469	656	1873	864	685	298	1123	1423	679	2537	1113
Box office	45	45	40	42	46	51	48	42	48	42	54	52	49	45	47	43	45	46
Base	1332	2475	504	747	1294	1208	1622	1545	660	1935	878	722	310	1175	1461	700	2605	1171
Foyer/lobby	35	35	40	33	35	35	37	33	38	33	36	47	55	38	34	33	35	36
Base	1317	2469	498	744	1274	1216	1631	1519	651	1901	874	730	314	1172	1452	692	2572	1185
Comfort of the auditorium	33	32	34	28	31	37	32	32	35	31	34	35	43	34	31	32	31	36
Base	1332	2485	494	742	1301	1224	1640	1532	655	1925	877	732	313	1181	1459	697	2596	1194
Comfort of the seating	25	24	28	19	22	29	25	24	25	24	23	25	31	28	22	22	23	28
Base	1267	2258	487	716	1206	1066	1526	1412	597	1773	819	671	297	1088	1351	664	2441	1056
Bars	19	19	20	16	21	20	21	19	17	19	19	25	26	20	18	21	19	19
Base	1140	2086	477	692	1109	907	1401	1258	568	1656	743	585	265	1003	1249	594	2259	937
Catering/ refreshments	13	14	18	11	13	14	14	13	14	13	15	17	16	15	12	14	13	14
Base	1200	2193	469	689	1142	1044	1448	1368	577	1710	766	658	282	1048	1294	636	2331	1031
Programme	25	27	34	22	25	28	24	28	25	27	21	35	32	30	24	24	25	30
Base	1303	2405	501	726	1259	1168	1596	1492	633	1863	852	715	309	1154	1423	673	2532	1149
Staff	48	48	48	44	48	50	48	47	49	45	51	55	52	50	47	42	47	49
Base	1272	2364	487	720	1222	1150	1563	1464	620	1821	821	717	305	1134	1401	659	2481	1122
Toilets	24	24	24	21	23	30	28	23	21	20	24	49	50	28	22	20	23	28
Base	1226	2296	437	688	1180	1166	1539	1398	583	1749	798	694	298	1096	1357	633	2379	1108
The performance	71	77	75	69	77	76	72	79	70	78	66	63	79	76	74	69	76	73
Base	1264	2337	460	709	1207	1173	1566	1439	599	1808	810	706	300	1121	1393	651	2443	1127
Value for money of your ticket	48	53	50	52	50	53	53	49	50	51	48	54	57	51	53	43	52	49
Base	1242	2320	454	684	1205	1165	1549	1425	589	1783	807	695	299	1108	1370	652	2414	1117
Overall enjoyment of your visit	56	66	61	55	66	65	61	66	59	64	55	60	71	66	61	56	62	64

Base: All who rated each aspect as very good.

*Performance Type key:

M = Musical

P = Play

O = Opera

D = Dance

NB: Entertainment type performances are not reported here due to the small base size

Satisfaction with a number of additional aspects was asked in the online survey. As toilets have consistently been an issue for many theatres, theatregoers were asked about the number of toilets available at the theatre they last visited. Only 18% rate this as very good, while 14% rate this as fairly poor and 7% as very poor. Women are more likely to rate the number of toilets available as poor overall (25% compared to 14% of men), younger visitors are also more likely to rate this aspect poorly (26% of those aged under 35).

Those who completed the main audience survey at a musical are likely to rate this poorly (27%), although this may be influenced by the fact that women make up a greater proportion of those seeing a musical.

As the chart above shows, the view of the stage is a crucial aspect of visiting the theatre – just over half (53%) rated their view of the stage as very good on their last visit to the theatre, while only 3% rated it as either fairly or very poor. Those attending a musical or a play when they completed the main survey are more likely to say this than those who saw a dance (55% and 54% compared to 42%).

In addition, the online survey also covered 'theatre facilities' as a whole. Overall, less than a quarter rated this as very good (22%); however, two in five rated this element as fairly good (43%), giving a combined 'good' score of 65%.

How would you rate each of the following at the theatre at which you saw your last performance?

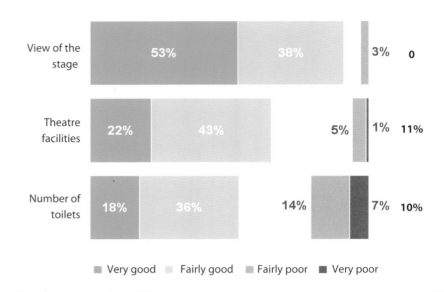

Base: All online survey respondents (716)

Source: Ipsos MORI

These results are fairly consistent across different groups of theatregoers, but those seeing an opera or dance performance when they completed the main survey are more positive about theatre facilities (82% and 89% good overall). This may be influenced by the fact that the major theatres for opera and dance are either grant aided or have received funding from (for example) the National Lottery in the last decade resulting in improved customer facilities.

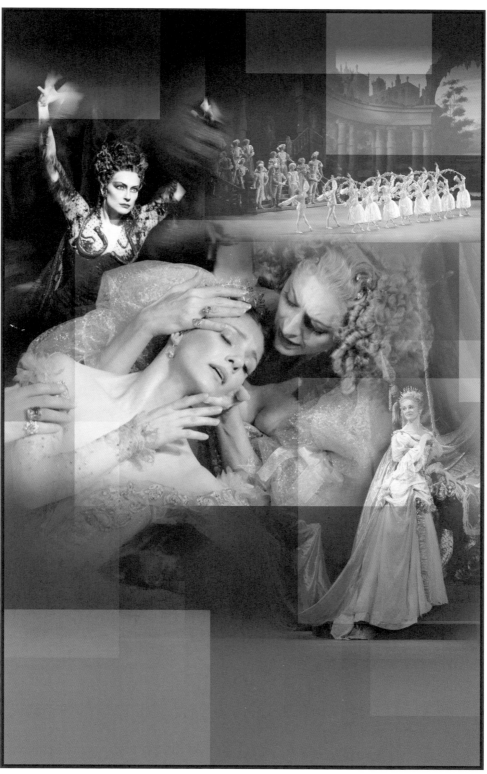

Sleeping Beauty

6 BOOKING TICKETS

Photographer: Carl O'Connell

WHEN WAS YOUR TICKET FOR TONIGHT'S PERFORMANCE BOOKED?

Around two thirds of theatregoers (63%) book tickets within one month of the performance. Of these, 19% book on the day of the performance and a further 23% within the week before the performance.

Compared to 2003 there has been a fall in the number of bookings made on the day of the performance from 27% to 19%, and overall 72% of audience members booked tickets within one month of the performance, again higher than the level seen in 2008. The results for 2003 are broadly consistent with those from 1997.

When was your ticket for this performance booked?

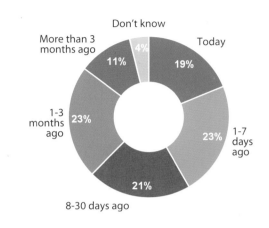

	2008 (%)	2003 (%)	1997 (%)
Today	19	27	21
1-7 days ago	23	21	20
8-30 days ago	21	23	22
1-3 months ago	23	19	26
More than 3 months ago	11	7	11
Don't know	4	2	

Base: All answering (2008: 4228, 2003: 6493, 1997: 6880)   Source: Ipsos MORI

- Younger theatregoers are more likely to book their ticket on the day of the performance (30% of those aged 16-24).

- Those aged 35+ are more likely to book their ticket in advance (36% of 35-54's and 40% of over 55's book more than a month in advance compared to 24% of 16-24's). This accentuates trends observed in 2003 and 1997.

- Overseas visitors, as might be expected, are more likely to book their ticket on the day of the performance compared to those from London (37% and 14% respectively). The higher proportion of younger visitors from overseas is likely to influence this, as is the likelihood of some tourists arriving in London and then deciding which shows to see.

- Overseas visitors are also more likely than average to use the official tkts booth in Leicester Square which sells on-the-day (and late availability) tickets.

- Theatregoers who are not working are more likely to book their ticket on the day of the performance (23%) perhaps reflecting a greater degree of flexibility around their leisure time.

- The bigger the party size, the longer the period between booking a ticket and the performance (for example some big groups such as coach parties may plan well ahead).

- Half of theatregoers (52%) attending in a group of five or more and nearly two thirds (63%) of those in organised groups book their ticket more than a month before the performance.

- This is contrasted by those going to the theatre alone, where just over four in ten (42%) book their ticket on the day of the performance.

- Half of tickets for both opera and dance performances were booked more than a month before the performance (54% and 55% respectively).

- This likely reflects the nature of ticketing of opera and dance; the major lyric theatres announce forthcoming productions in 'seasons'. Once booking opens for a new season, there is a flurry of bookings from regular customers, many for performances some time into the future.

- Those seeing a play are more likely to have bought their ticket 1 – 7 days before the performance (29%) or within one month of the performance (72% compared to 63% overall).

- Those seeing a musical are more likely than those seeing either an opera or a dance performance to buy their ticket both 1 – 7 days before the performance (23%) and within a month of the performance (63%).

WHEN WAS YOUR TICKET FOR THIS PERFORMANCE BOOKED?

	Gender %		Age %				Origin %			*Performance Type %				Income %			Working Status %	
	M	F	16-24	25-34	35-54	55+	London	Rest of UK	Overseas	M	P	O	D	Up to £20,000	£20,001 - £50,000	£50,001+	Working	Not Working
Base	1402	2630	528	780	1352	1313	1743	1666	741	2127	958	764	325	1236	1531	735	2722	1277
Today	23	18	30	19	17	17	14	15	37	20	20	8	8	23	18	17	18	23
Yesterday	6	5	7	6	5	5	4	4	12	5	7	2	2	4	5	7	6	5
2-3 days ago	6	7	8	8	7	5	8	5	9	7	8	4	4	6	7	7	7	6
4-7 days ago	11	11	8	14	11	9	14	10	6	11	14	7	8	10	13	10	12	9
8-30 days ago	21	20	14	24	21	22	26	20	14	20	23	21	19	18	24	23	22	18
1-3 months ago	21	24	17	22	25	25	22	29	14	22	19	33	41	23	22	25	23	23
More than 3 months ago	9	11	6	6	12	15	8	16	5	11	5	21	15	12	10	8	10	10
Don't know/can't remember	3	4	10	3	2	2	5	2	4	4	4	4	3	5	2	3	3	5
1-7 days	24	23	23	28	23	19	26	18	27	23	29	13	15	20	24	24	24	21
Within 1 month	67	61	66	70	62	58	66	53	78	63	72	42	42	61	66	64	64	62
More than 1 month ago	30	36	24	27	36	40	29	45	18	33	25	54	55	34	32	33	34	33

*Performance Type key:

M = Musical

P = Play

O = Opera

D = Dance

NB: Entertainment type performances are not reported here due to the small base size

- As might be expected, those for whom the theatre was the main reason for visiting London are more likely to book their ticket more than a month in advance (53% compared to 17% of those for whom the theatre was not an important factor for visiting).

Theatregoers in the online survey were asked how far in advance they book theatre tickets generally. It is important to state that respondents were asked this generally and answers are not necessarily specific to theatre visits in the West End. More than half report generally booking tickets within one month of the performance and a similar amount more than one month in advance (46%).

One in ten of those taking part in the online survey tend to book their ticket on the day of a performance (9%) and a further 13% book a week prior to a performance.

- These results suggest that, when thinking about the theatre generally, audience members believe that they do plan ahead for their visit (in the main audience survey those booking more than a month in advance is just 34% compared to the 46% who say they generally book more than a month ahead in the online survey).

One sixth of male theatregoers responding to the online survey (16%) tend to book their ticket on the day of a performance, this compared to 6% of females. Further, half of female theatregoers (49%) book their ticket more than a month before a performance, compared to 41% of males. This suggests more advance planning on the part of female theatregoers.

When did you book your theatre tickets for the last show you went to see?
And generally how far in advance do you book your theatre tickets?

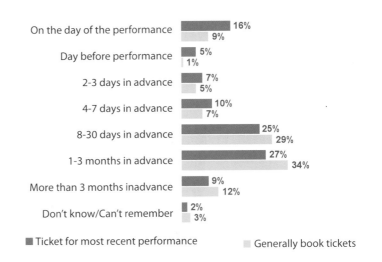

	Ticket for most recent performance	Generally book tickets
On the day of the performance	16%	9%
Day before performance	5%	1%
2-3 days in advance	7%	5%
4-7 days in advance	10%	7%
8-30 days in advance	25%	29%
1-3 months in advance	27%	34%
More than 3 months in advance	9%	12%
Don't know/Can't remember	2%	3%

Base: All online respondents (716)

Source: Ipsos MORI

- Over half of theatregoers aged 55+ in the online survey (55%) book their tickets more than a month in advance of a performance, and younger theatregoers as we have seen are more likely to book last minute.

- Half of audience members who completed the main survey at an opera (55%) or dance (56%) performance tend to book tickets more than a month in advance, again consistent with behaviour seen in the main audience survey.

Hairspray

HOW TICKET WAS BOOKED

Since 2003 there has been a large increase in the number of theatregoers using the internet to book tickets. Around half (48%) use the internet (in a variety of locations) to purchase tickets, compared to just 17% in the previous survey.

Less than one third (29%) of theatregoers book their ticket in person and just 18% book their ticket over the phone. This marks a decrease from 2003 when both figures were 38%. This clearly reflects the increasing use of the internet for booking tickets.

- Half of female theatregoers (50%) book their ticket online compared to 46% of men. One third of males (33%) book their ticket in person, this being slightly higher than the percentage of women using this method (27%).

- Audience members aged 25-34 are most likely to book their ticket online (59%), followed by those aged 35-54 (51%). Those aged over 55 are the least likely to book online (39%).

  - The youngest theatregoers (aged 16-24) are more likely to book their tickets in person (37%) and less likely to book online (42% compared to 59% for 25-34 year olds and 51% for 35-54 year olds).

  - This could be seen as surprising given the received wisdom that the younger generations are more 'techno-savvy' than their older counterparts. A 'leave it till late' attitude to booking tickets among the young would also favour sales in person at either ticket booths (e.g. tkts) or at theatre box offices.

How was your ticket for this performance booked?

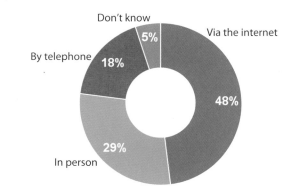

	2008 (%)	2003 (%)
Via the internet	48	17
In person	29	38
By telephone	18	38
Don't know	5	6

Base: All answering: (2008: 4151, 2003: 6334)   Source: Ipsos MORI

How was your ticket for this performance booked?

Showing breakdown of internet bookings

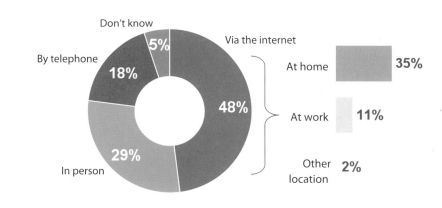

Base: All answering: (4151)   Source: Ipsos MORI

  - Older theatregoers are more likely to book by telephone (25%).

- Amongst UK based theatregoers, around half (52%) use the internet to book their ticket, whereas a similar proportion of overseas visitors (50%) book their ticket in person. This likely reflects the fact that domestic visitors are more familiar with where tickets can be booked online (and also more likely to book their ticket in advance) and could reflect some reluctance on the part of overseas visitors to purchase tickets which must be collected at the theatre (tickets are almost never posted overseas).

- If we look at only those booking via the internet, 73% booked their ticket using the internet at home, 23% used the internet at work and 4% used the internet at another location.

- Half of theatregoers who attend a performance with one other person (53%) or two/three others (50%) in the party use the internet to book tickets.

  - For those visiting the theatre alone, half (53%) book in person and one third (33%) book online.

  - Larger parties of 5 or more and organised groups book their ticket by telephone (24% and 32% respectively).

- Over eight in ten (83%) tickets booked on the day of a performance are done so in person, whereas just one in sixteen (6%) are booked online.

  - For tickets booked more than a month prior to the performance, three in five (60%) book on the internet with 46% doing so at home.

- More than three in five theatregoers at a dance performance book their tickets online (65%).

  - Those seeing a play are more likely to book by telephone (23%) than attendees at other genres.

  - More tickets for musicals (29%) and plays (30%) are booked in person than for opera (25%) and dance (19%).

How did you book the ticket for the last show you went to see? And generally how do you book your theatre tickets?

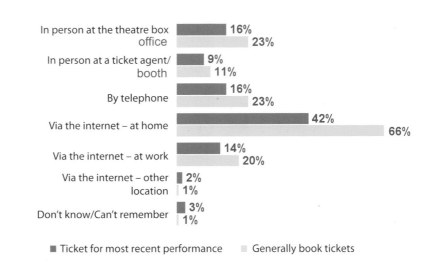

Base: All respondents (716)   Source: Ipsos MORI

Those taking part in the online survey were also asked about how they book theatre tickets generally. These results contrast from what we saw when asking theatregoers about one particular performance only (although again it is important to remember that theatregoers may not be thinking solely about going to the theatre in London when considering this).

One third of theatregoers (34%) book their tickets in person – 23% of these at the theatre box office and a further 11% at a ticket agent/booth. A quarter (23%) book their tickets by telephone.

The use of the internet to book tickets among this group is high with four fifths doing so (79%), of which 66% do so at home and a further 20% at work. This is higher than the proportion saying they used the internet when asked about the ticket for the specific performance, underlining that the internet is now very much seen as a main way to book tickets.

- As with the self-completion questionnaire, younger theatregoers aged 16-34 are more likely to book their ticket online than those aged 55+ (82% and 73% respectively).

- Similarly, one third of those aged 55+ (34%) generally book their ticket by telephone, and a further 27% at the theatre box office.

- Those who have attended the theatre most frequently in the last year are more likely to generally book either at the theatre box office (32%) or by telephone (30%).

HOW WAS YOUR TICKET FOR THIS PERFORMANCE BOOKED?

	Gender %		Age %				Origin %			*Performance Type %				Income %			Working Status %	
	M	F	16-24	25-34	35-54	55+	London	Rest of UK	Overseas	M	P	O	D	Up to £20,000	£20,001 - £50,000	£50,001+	Working	Not Working
Base	1377	2589	521	780	1334	1276	1717	1633	723	2111	942	724	322	1219	1506	729	2691	1247
Via the internet - from home	34	36	32	34	39	32	33	43	25	36	29	39	46	36	37	34	37	32
In person (you or someone else)	33	27	37	25	26	31	24	23	50	29	30	25	19	33	26	25	26	36
By telephone	17	18	11	13	18	25	19	20	11	17	23	19	11	17	16	21	17	18
Via the internet – from work	10	12	7	23	11	5	17	9	6	10	12	9	17	6	17	13	15	3
Via the internet – at another location	2	2	3	1	1	2	1	2	2	2	1	1	1	2	1	1	2	2
Don't know/can't remember	5	5	10	3	5	4	6	4	6	5	5	6	5	7	3	5	4	8
Internet	46	50	42	59	51	39	51	53	34	49	42	50	65	44	55	49	53	38

*Performance Type key:

M = Musical
P = Play
O = Opera
D = Dance
NB: Entertainment type performances are not reported here due to the small base size

SOURCES FROM WHICH THE TICKET WAS BOOKED

In 2008 a third of theatregoers (36%) booked their ticket through the theatre box office, a drop from 2003 when this was half (51%). Three in ten (31%) booked tickets through a website, either the show/theatre's website (16%), or another website (15%). Use of both these types of website has doubled since 2003. This change is even more stark when compared to 1997, where just 1% of theatregoers mentioned booking their ticket by computer including email and intranet. It is likely that the increasing use of the internet has to a great extent caused the fall in theatregoers booking through the box office.

From which one of these sources was your ticket for this performance booked?

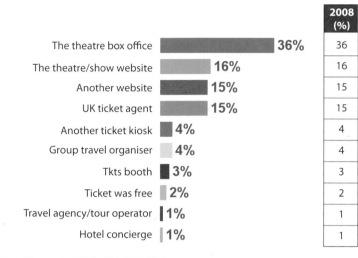

	2008 (%)	2003 (%)
The theatre box office	36	51
The theatre/show website	16	7
Another website	15	6
UK ticket agent	15	13
Another ticket kiosk	4	5
Group travel organiser	4	6
Tkts booth	3	5
Ticket was free	2	1
Travel agency/tour operator	1	1
Hotel concierge	1	3

Base: All answering (2008: 4090, 2003: 6424)   Source: Ipsos MORI

UK based ticket agencies (15%), ticket kiosks (4%), group travel organisers (4%) and the tkts booth in Leicester Square (3%) are other sources used to book tickets. These methods of booking have remained more or less consistent with the results seen in 2003.

• Amongst those booking through the theatre box office, 49% did so in person and 30% over the telephone. In fact telephone bookings, taken by box office staff located in a specific theatre are relatively rare nowadays; most calls are taken by a theatre group's central phone booking operation and/or an appointed third party agent.

• The theatre box office is used by four in ten (41%) male theatregoers to book tickets.

As we saw before female theatregoers are more likely to book tickets over the internet, nearly one in five (17%) book on the theatre/show's website and a further 16% book on another website such as Lastminute.com (theatregoers were asked to specify which other websites they had used if mentioning another website).

• Just under half of those aged over 55 purchase their ticket directly from the theatre box office (45% compared to just 27% of 25-34 year olds).

- Over 55's are also more likely to have used a group travel organiser to book their ticket (5% compared to 2% of those aged 16-24).

- Those aged 25-34 are most likely to use a website other than the show or theatre website to book their ticket (26%).

- Theatregoers aged 16-24 are more inclined to use a ticket kiosk other than the tkts booth (6%).

• Domestic visitors are more likely to use either the show or theatre website or another website to book their ticket (both 17%).

- Overseas visitors tend to use ticket booths – both tkts (7%) and other booths (12%).

- As you may expect overseas visitors are more likely to use either a hotel concierge (3%) or an overseas ticket agency to book a ticket (1%).

• Three in five theatregoers who attend a performance alone book their ticket through the theatre box office (57%) or via the show/theatre's website (14%). By contrast just under half (45%) of parties with more than five people use third party sources – the most popular being a group travel organiser (13%) and UK ticket agents (16%).

- Six in ten (60%) day of the performance bookings are made through the theatre box office, whilst 15% are booked at a ticket kiosk other than tkts and another 12% through the tkts booth in Leicester Square.

- Half of all tickets booked for both plays (51%) and opera (59%) are booked through the theatre box office.

  - Half (51%) of bookings to musicals use a third party source. Tickets for these performances are often those advertised and can be seen offered at discount prices by ticket agents.

  - Websites other than the show/theatre website are often used (17%), as are UK ticket agents (19%), ticket kiosks (5%) and tkts booth (3%) to book tickets for musicals.

- Looking specifically at websites other than the show/theatre website, overall just over one sixth (15%) of theatregoers book their ticket on another website. This is more than double the proportion using this source in 2003.

  - Within this, less than one in ten (8%) book on Lastminute.com and a further 3% book on Ticketmaster. Theatregoers also cite numerous other websites as the source of their ticket; these include gift websites and tourism sites. The range of sites mentioned indicates both the number of options out there for booking tickets and that there does not seem to be an overwhelming market leader.

Which, if any, of the following websites have you used in the last 12 months to book theatre tickets?

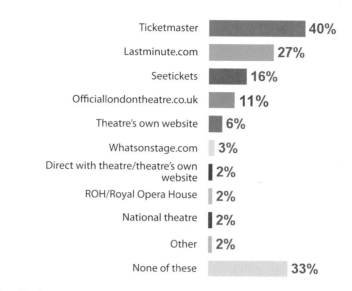

Ticketmaster	40%
Lastminute.com	27%
Seetickets	16%
Officiallondontheatre.co.uk	11%
Theatre's own website	6%
Whatsonstage.com	3%
Direct with theatre/theatre's own website	2%
ROH/Royal Opera House	2%
National theatre	2%
Other	2%
None of these	33%

Base: All online survey respondents (716)   Source: Ipsos MORI

In the online questionnaire, theatregoers were asked about various SOLT initiatives including the tkts booth in Leicester Square (and Brent Cross). Nearly half (45%) are aware of this. Of those aware, nearly two fifths (38%) have used tkts in the past to book their ticket.

Respondents were also asked in further detail about the websites they have used to book tickets in the past twelve months. Two fifths (40%) have used Ticketmaster, a further quarter (27%) Lastminute.com and 16% used Seetickets. These results are higher than those seen in the self completion, paper questionnaire as this question relates to any theatre performance in the past twelve months.

Eleven per cent have used the SOLT website (officiallondontheatre.co.uk), and a further 6% have booked their ticket through a theatre's own website.

- Within this the most cited are the Royal Opera House (2%), National Theatre (2%) and English National Opera (1%)[7].

Younger theatregoers aged 16-34, are more likely to have used sites such as Ticketmaster (44%), compared to those aged 55+ (31%). Similar trends are evident in usage of Lastminute.com (36% and 15% respectively).

- As would be expected, those aged 55+ are more likely to have not used a website to book tickets (42%) than those aged between 16 and 34 (31%).

Fourteen per cent of theatregoers who completed the main audience survey at an opera performance have used a theatre's own website to book a ticket in the past twelve months.

7   It is worth noting that these websites are often the main (and, in some instances, the only) sites from which to make online bookings for productions from these organisations (i.e. online ticket agents do not sell tickets for many productions from these theatres).

FROM WHICH ONE OF THESE SOURCES WAS YOUR TICKET FOR THIS PERFORMANCE BOOKED?

	Gender %		Age %				Origin %			*Performance Type %				Income %			Working Status %	
	M	F	16-24	25-34	35-54	55+	London	Rest of UK	Overseas	M	P	O	D	Up to £20,000	£20,001 - £50,000	£50,001+	Working	Not Working
Base	1373	2545	526	764	1314	1259	1693	1604	718	2060	931	732	314	1212	1488	712	2642	1249
The theatre box office	41	34	36	27	34	45	41	30	39	29	51	59	40	37	33	39	33	43
The show or theatre website	14	17	14	17	16	16	17	16	12	12	17	30	36	14	17	19	16	15
Another website	13	16	15	26	15	7	19	15	8	17	11	2	12	13	19	9	18	9
A UK ticket agent	14	15	11	14	17	14	10	22	7	19	7	1	4	16	15	16	16	10
Another ticket kiosk	6	3	6	5	3	3	1	2	12	5	2	-	*	4	4	3	4	5
Via a group travel organiser	3	4	2	3	3	5	1	6	4	5	1	*	3	4	3	3	3	6
The tkts ticket booth in Leicester Square	3	3	3	3	3	3	1	2	7	3	2	*	*	3	3	2	3	3
Ticket was free	1	2	2	2	1	1	3	1	*	1	3	*		2	1	2	2	2
A travel agency or tour operator	*	1	1	1	1	1	*	1	2	1	*	*	-	1	1	*	1	2
A hotel concierge	1	1	1	1	1	1	-	*	3	1	1	-	*	*	1	2	1	1
An overseas ticket agency	*	*	*	*	1	1	*	*	1	*	1	*	*	*	*	1	*	1
A tout/scalper (selling in the street)	-	*	-	-	*	-	-	-	*	*	-	-	-	-	-	*	-	*
Other	2	2	1	2	2	2	3	2	1	2	2	3	*	2	2	2	2	2
Don't know/can't remember	3	3	6	2	3	2	3	3	3	3	4	3	3	4	2	2	3	4
Via a third party	39	42	39	49	44	33	32	48	44	51	23	4	20	41	43	35	43	35
Direct	55	50	50	44	50	61	59	46	51	42	67	89	77	52	50	59	50	58
Online ticket agency	11	13	13	22	12	4	15	12	6	14	9	1	10	11	16	6	14	8

*Performance Type key:

M = Musical

P = Play

O = Opera

D = Dance

NB: Entertainment type performances are not reported here due to the small base size

We Will Rock You

FULL PRICE OR DISCOUNTED TICKETS?

Just under half of all theatregoers (47%) purchased their ticket at full price, with 42% purchasing at a discount/ reduced price. This marks a change from 2003 when more than half (54%) bought their ticket at full price, with discounted/reduced sales at 37%. Four per cent state their ticket was free, and a further 7% do not know if it was full price or discounted.

These figures seem to confirm the generally held view that a higher proportion of discounted or reduced price tickets are being sold then ever before.

The category 'don't know' of course comprises some who bought tickets at full price, and others who bought at discount. This would swell the responses for the other categories by a few percentage points.

- Fifty six per cent of those aged 55+ paid full price for their ticket, compared to 38% of those between the ages of 16 and 24. Those aged 25-34 are the most likely to have bought their ticket at a reduced or discounted price (51%).

- Younger theatregoers (16-24 year olds) are more likely than other age groups to say their ticket was free (7%) or that they did not know how much it was (12%).

  - Theatregoers within this age group are attending with friends (38%), other family members (33%) or as part of an organised group (10%), so therefore might not be involved in the ticket buying process.

Was your ticket...?

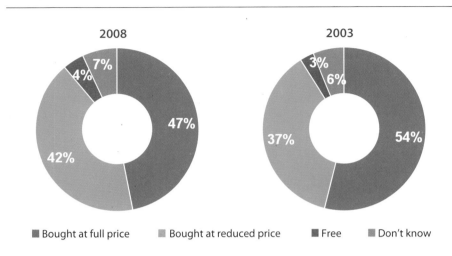

Base: All answering (2008: 4150, 2003: 6466)   Source: Ipsos MORI

- Half of theatregoers from London (47%) bought their ticket at a reduced or discounted price, whereas a large number of those from elsewhere in the UK (53%) and overseas (50%) bought their ticket at full price.

- London theatregoers are possibly more aware of the discounts available and where to find these. Those from outside London may have bought tickets in advance at full price, or do not know where to source discounted tickets.

- Nearly seven in ten in an organised group (67%) bought their ticket at a reduced or discounted price. Conversely, those visiting alone (58%) and with another person (50%) bought their ticket at full price.

- As we saw with younger theatregoers, one fifth (19%) of those in an organised group do not know what price was paid for their ticket.

- Nearly three fifths of on the day ticket purchases (56%) are at a reduced or discounted price. On the other hand, a similar number (60%), booking tickets more than a month in advance paid full price for their tickets.

- Nearly three fifths of those earning in excess of £50,000 (58%) have paid full price.

- Two thirds of theatregoers attending either an opera or dance performance (67%) paid full price for their ticket. Around half of those attending a musical (46%) and three quarters an entertainment production (73%) bought their ticket at a reduced or discounted price.

- Audience members at a larger theatre are more likely to have paid full price for their ticket (52%).

WAS YOUR TICKET...?

	Gender %		Age %				Origin %			*Performance Type %				Income %			Working Status %	
	M	F	16-24	25-34	35-54	55+	London	Rest of UK	Overseas	M	P	O	D	Up to £20,000	£20,001 - £50,000	£50,001+	Working	Not Working
Base	1389	2588	525	757	1339	1295	1722	1635	717	2087	928	759	322	1229	1510	723	2689	1256
Bought at full price	50	46	38	40	49	56	41	53	50	44	53	67	67	43	47	58	47	47
Bought at a reduced or discounted price	40	44	42	51	42	37	47	39	40	46	35	28	25	44	46	33	44	40
Free	3	4	7	4	3	3	7	2	1	3	7	2	3	5	4	4	4	4
Don't know	6	7	12	6	6	4	5	6	9	7	5	3	5	8	4	6	5	9
Reduced/ Discounted/ Free	44	48	50	55	45	40	54	41	41	49	42	30	28	48	49	36	48	44

*Performance Type key:
M = Musical
P = Play
O = Opera
D = Dance
NB: Entertainment type performances are not reported here due to the small base size

IF THE TICKET WAS NOT FULL PRICE, WOULD THEATREGOERS STILL HAVE COME?

One third of theatregoers (32%) who did not pay full price for their ticket state they definitely would not have come to the theatre if it had been full price.

Two fifths are more positive (39%) and say they might not have come and 22% are definite that they would have come anyway. Seven percent say they do not know or that it depends.

In 2003, two thirds (64%) stated if the ticket was full price they would definitely or might not have come, this compared to 71% in 2008. Whilst we cannot be sure, this suggests that price is a stronger motivating factor in 2008 than it was in 2003.

- Nearly two fifths of male theatregoers (37%) state they definitely would not have come if they had to pay full price, this compares to 31% of women.

- Although generally age does not impact on intentions to visit, the only notable exception is that nearly three in ten (27%) theatregoers aged 55+ state that they would have come anyway.

- Nearly two fifths (38%) of theatregoers from London say they definitely would not have come to the theatre if their ticket was full price. This drops to 25% of overseas theatregoers.

Would you have come if you had to pay full price for a ticket?

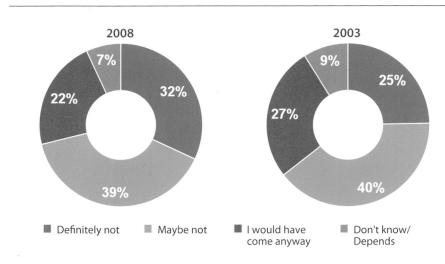

Base: All answering who did not pay full price (2008: 1722, 2003: 2588)   Source: Ipsos MORI

- Over a third (36%) of those booking a ticket on the day of the performance would definitely not have come if they had to pay full price. This suggests perhaps theatregoers are aware of discounted tickets and their availability and see no reason to purchase at full price.

- As would be expected, the highest earners state they would still come to the theatre regardless of cost (28% of those earning £50,000 or more) compared to 21% of those earning up to £20,000.

- Interestingly, amongst those for whom going to the theatre was their main reason for visiting London, 44% might not have come if their ticket had been full price.

- Audience members at a dance performance are most likely to say they would not have come if they had to pay full price (48% compared to just 28% for those seeing a play).

PLEASE INDICATE WHICH ONE OF THESE STATEMENTS BEST DESCRIBES YOUR SITUATION

	Gender %		Age %				Origin %			*Performance Type %				Income %			Working Status %	
	M	F	16-24	25-34	35-54	55+	London	Rest of UK	Overseas	M	P	O	D	Up to £20,000	£20,001-£50,000	£50,001+	Working	Not Working
Base	535	1137	254	396	552	446	789	611	286	1003	387	210	84	548	675	237	1175	489
I definitely would not have come if I'd had to pay full price	37	31	30	36	34	30	38	29	25	32	28	36	48	36	31	32	33	32
I might not have come if I'd had to pay full price	35	40	38	40	40	37	37	43	35	39	41	31	29	37	42	34	39	39
I would have come anyway	22	22	24	18	20	27	17	23	30	22	21	24	16	21	20	28	21	23
Don't know/depends	6	7	8	6	6	6	7	5	10	7	10	9	7	5	7	6	7	6
Definitely/Might not have come	72	71	68	76	74	67	75	72	60	71	69	67	77	74	73	65	71	71

*Performance Type key:
M = Musical
P = Play
O = Opera
D = Dance
NB: Entertainment type performances are not reported here due to the small base size

7 BOOKING FEES

RAZZLE
DAZZLE

CHICAGO
THE MUSICAL

CHICAGO

CAMBRIDGE THEATRE

'STILL THE HOTTEST SHOW IN TOWN'

Now starring
BONNIE LANGFORD
as Roxie Hart

Those taking part in the online survey were asked a number of questions around booking fees and fees in general to assess their attitudes towards these and whether they impact on purchasing behaviour.

UNDERSTANDING OF BOOKING FEES

Just 5% of theatregoers completing the online survey strongly agree that they understand why a booking fee is charged. A quarter (26%) tend to agree with the statement but similar proportions both tend to disagree and strongly disagree.

It is clear that understanding of booking fees is fairly limited and it appears that this lack of understanding may impact on some attitudes towards booking fees.

To what extent do you agree, or disagree, with the following statements? I understand why a booking fee is charged.

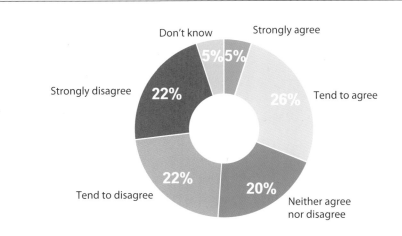

Base: All online survey respondents (716)   Source: Ipsos MORI

LEVELS OF BOOKING FEES

Theatregoers taking part in the online survey are sceptical about the level of booking fees – only 1% strongly agree that booking fees are currently at about the right level, and fewer than one in ten agree at all (9%). Almost three in five disagree that booking fees are at the right level (58%).

To what extent do you agree, or disagree, with the following statements? Booking fees are currently at about the right level.

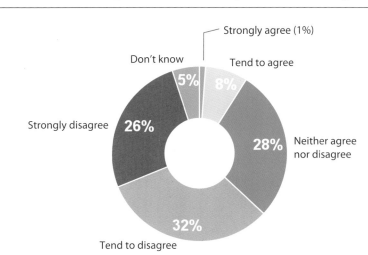

Base: All online survey respondents (716)   Source: Ipsos MORI

HOW BOOKING FEES ARE CALCULATED

Twenty seven per cent of those taking part in the online survey agree that booking fees should be calculated as a percentage of the ticket price rather than be a standard charge. Thirty eight per cent disagree with this statement and the remainder are either neutral or don't know.

- Those earning a lower annual income (up to £20,000) are more likely than those earning the most to agree that fees should be a percentage of the price (34% compared to 20%).

To what extent do you agree, or disagree, with the following statements? Where a booking fee is charged, it should be calculated as a percentage of the ticket price rather than be a standard charge.

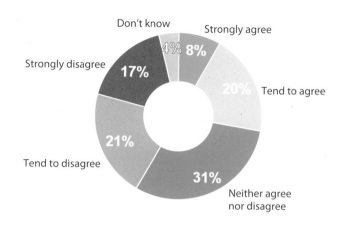

Base: All online survey respondents (716)　　　Source: Ipsos MORI

HOW MUCH DO THEATREGOERS PAY IN BOOKING FEES?

Theatregoers estimate that they pay £2.69 per ticket on average in booking fees[8]. Fifteen per cent of theatregoers taking part in the online survey estimate that they pay more than £4 per ticket in fees. Thirteen per cent of theatregoers are unable to say how much they pay for booking fees on average suggesting that as well as confusion over why they are charged there is confusion over the amount.

- Those who attend the theatre less frequently are more likely to say they don't know how much they pay for booking fees (27%) compared to those who attend the theatre more frequently (9%).

When booking a ticket and paying a booking fee what, on average, do you think you normally pay as a booking fee? And what do you think is an acceptable level for a booking fee?

	Average paid booking fee	Acceptable level of booking fee
Average	£2.69	£1.31
£0.01 - £2.00	29%	75%
£2.01 - £4.00	43%	11%
£4.01 - £5.00	11%	1%
£5.01 - £10.00	3%	0%
£10.01 - £15.00	0%	0%
£15.01+	0%	0%

Base: All online survey respondents (716)　　　Source: Ipsos MORI

8　This figure is an average calculated from the range of responses in the survey.

WHAT IS CONSIDERED AN ACCEPTABLE BOOKING FEE?

Three quarters of theatregoers completing the online survey feel that an amount between £0.00 and £2.00 is an acceptable level for a booking fee. On average, a booking fee of £1.30 is seen as acceptable.

• Those who visit the theatre less frequently find a slightly higher booking fee acceptable (£1.50 compared to £1.20).

• Overall, one in ten don't know what an acceptable level of booking fees is - this increases for men (21%) and those aged over 55 (21%).

INCORPORATING BOOKING FEES INTO THE COST OF THE TICKET

More than half of theatregoers taking part in the online survey (56%) agree that they would like to see booking fees incorporated into the cost of a ticket rather than be shown separately. Just a quarter disagree with this suggestion. This is a change to booking fees that clearly has support among a proportion of theatregoers – however this is by no means unanimous.

• Men are more likely to be in favour of this option (64% agree compared to 51% of women).

To what extent do you agree, or disagree, with the following statements? I would rather any booking fee was incorporated into the cost of the ticket, rather than be shown separately.

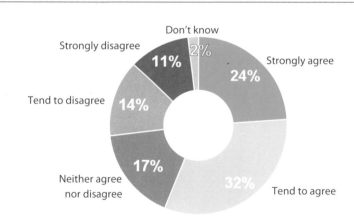

Base: All online survey respondents (716)   Source: Ipsos MORI

BOOKING FEES AND MULTIPLE TICKET BUYING

When buying more than one ticket, there is a feeling that only one booking fee should be charged. More than nine in ten theatregoers completing the online survey agree that there should only be one booking fee when buying multiple tickets (93%), of which 73% strongly agree with this. Only 2% disagree with this statement.

To what extent do you agree, or disagree, with the following statements?

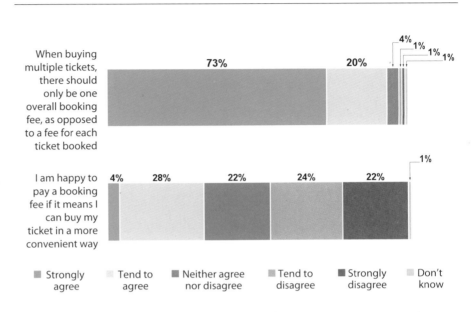

Base: All online survey respondents (716)

Source: Ipsos MORI

To what extent do you agree, or disagree, with the following statements?

	When buying multiple tickets, there should only be one overall booking fee, as opposed to a fee for each ticket booked	I am happy to pay a booking fee if it means I can buy my ticket in a more convenient way
Strongly agree	73%	4%
Tend to agree	20%	28%
Neither	4%	22%
Tend to disagree	1%	24%
Strongly disagree	1%	22%
Don't know	1%	1%

Base: All online survey respondents (716)

Source: Ipsos MORI

BOOKING FEES AND METHODS OF TICKET BUYING

Thirty one per cent of theatregoers completing the online survey agree that they would be happy to pay a booking fee if it means they can book their ticket in a more convenient way. However, 45% disagree with this – presumably feeling that they should be able to book in whichever way they want without paying a booking fee.

Aida. Photographer: Tristram Kenton

THE INFLUENCE OF BOOKING FEES ON TICKET BUYING

Half of theatregoers taking part in the online survey agree that the presence of a booking fee influences their ticket buying. Within this group 18% strongly agree and 35% tend to agree. One in five theatregoers in the online survey disagree with this statement (21%), with most tending to disagree (16%). A quarter of respondents are neutral on this – stating that they neither agree nor disagree.

To what extent do you agree, or disagree, with the following statements?

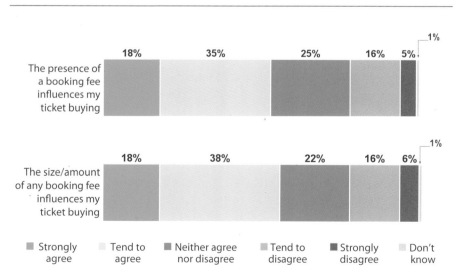

The presence of a booking fee influences my ticket buying: 18% | 35% | 25% | 16% | 5% | 1%

The size/amount of any booking fee influences my ticket buying: 18% | 38% | 22% | 16% | 6% | 1%

- ■ Strongly agree
- ■ Tend to agree
- ■ Neither agree nor disagree
- ■ Tend to disagree
- ■ Strongly disagree
- ■ Don't know

Base: All online survey respondents (716)

Source: Ipsos MORI

THE SIZE OF THE BOOKING FEE AND TICKET BUYING

More than half of theatregoers completing the online survey agree that the size/amount of any booking fee influences their ticket buying, with more tending to agree (38%).

This is a similar response to that which we saw when asking theatregoers about the presence of a booking fee influencing their ticket buying. This perhaps suggests that it is the addition of a booking fee that has more impact than the actual level of this fee.

Avenue Q

AWARENESS OF TRANSACTION FEES

Just under half of theatregoers taking part in the online survey (45%) are aware that you may be charged a transaction fee when purchasing theatre tickets over the telephone or internet, in addition to per ticket booking fees.

Sometimes, when you book tickets over the phone/via the internet, you will be charged a transaction fee in addition to any booking fee(s). To what extent are you aware of this?

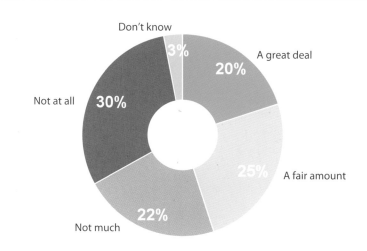

Base: All online survey respondents (716)   Source: Ipsos MORI

SHOULD THEATREGOERS BE CHARGED A BOOKING FEE AND A TRANSACTION FEE?

As might be expected almost all theatregoers completing the online survey agree that they should not be charged a transaction fee if they have paid a booking fee. The strength of feeling about this is shown by the four in five (81%) who strongly agree with the statement.

To what extent do you agree or disagree with the following statement. If I have paid a booking fee, I should not be charged a transaction fee.

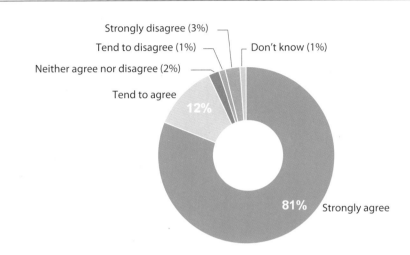

Base: All online survey respondents (716)

Source: Ipsos MORI

RESTORATION LEVIES

In order to help meet the significant costs of large-scale repair and refurbishment work, some West End commercial theatres have introduced a 'restoration levy' on each ticket sold. Theatregoers were asked about their awareness of, and views on, theatre restoration and levies to help pay for it.

Firstly, theatregoers taking part in the online survey were asked about how restoration is currently funded.

Three quarters (75%) of theatregoers believe that theatre companies or owners fund restoration of theatres, three in five (63%) think that the National Lottery contributes and a quarter think both local government (26%) or national government (24%) contribute to this. Fifteen percent do not know who contributes to restoration.

The incorrect assumption that public money has been or is being used to help fund West End commercial theatre restoration work (via the National Lottery or government agencies) is of interest in the context of the ongoing debate on this topic.

A number of West End theatres are in need of repair/restoration. Which of the following organisations do you think contribute towards funding these restorations?

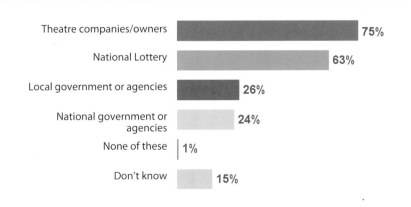

Base: All online survey respondents (716)

Source: Ipsos MORI

AWARENESS OF THE RESTORATION LEVY

Just 9% of theatregoers completing the online survey state they are very aware of restoration levies, and 15% are fairly aware meaning that only a quarter (24%) have some awareness of this approach. Almost three in five (58%) are not at all aware of the levy and when combined with those who are not very aware of the levy this rises to three quarters (74%).

This low level of awareness will perhaps, in part, be attributable to the fact that, when this research was carried out, theatres which imposed a restoration levy were in the minority (more do so today). However, it also suggests that some people are paying a restoration levy without being aware of doing so.

- Those who visit the theatre in London most often have a higher level of awareness of the levy (40%) and correspondingly those who visit least often have a lower awareness (92% are not aware of the levy).

A number of theatres are charging a 'restoration levy' as part of the ticket price to help with the restoration of West End theatres. To what extent are you aware of this practice?

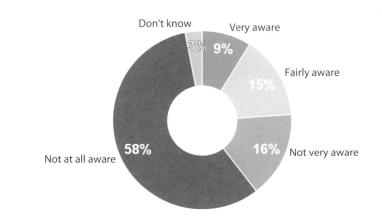

Base: All online survey respondents (716)

Source: Ipsos MORI

Mamma Mia!

WILLINGNESS TO PAY A RESTORATION LEVY

Despite low awareness of the restoration levy, theatregoers in the online survey are not averse to paying this kind of levy. Almost three in five (57%) would be willing to pay a restoration levy as part of the price of their theatre ticket. Just 9% would not be at all willing to pay a levy, though 29% are not very willing.

And overall, how willing would you be to pay a 'restoration levy' as part of your theatre ticket price?

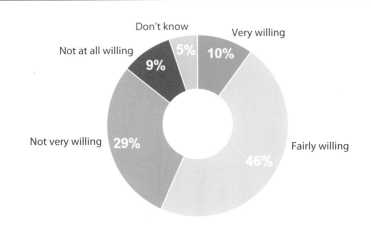

Base: All online survey respondents (716)   Source: Ipsos MORI

HOW MUCH SHOULD THE RESTORATION LEVY BE?

When asked how much the restoration levy should be, theatregoers in the online survey suggested an average amount of £1.16.

Half of theatregoers taking part in the online survey (48%) feel that levy should be between £0.01 and £1.00 and a quarter (27%) think it should be between £1.00 and £2.00. Only 14% think it should be more than £2.00.

- Those earning more than £50,000 suggest a higher average amount for the restoration levy at £1.36.

If a 'restoration levy' was introduced, what do you think it should be set at per ticket?

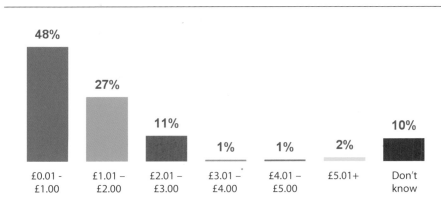

Base: All online survey respondents (716)   Source: Ipsos MORI

BOOKING FEES, TRANSACTION FEES AND RESTORATION LEVIES: SOME CONCLUSIONS.

The in-depth probing of attitudes to ticketing fees among the online respondents to our survey reveals, as ever, a range of attitudes. However, some general points seem to emerge.

It appears that some theatergoers would prefer not to have to pay booking fees or transaction fees – and, where they do apply, would prefer them to be as low as possible. It would, of course, be highly surprising were this to be otherwise since many of the questions boil down to 'Would you like to pay less for your tickets?'

However, of interest is the acceptance of and preparedness to pay restoration levies (this contrasts to booking fees and particularly transaction fees which some theatergoers do not feel should both be charged). This is likely to be to do with understanding; the case for restoration levies is largely understood. Even if theatre-specific reasons (e.g. the need for more foyer space at Theatre X, air conditioning at Theatre Y) have not been made, the general concept of helping to improve theatre infrastructure seems to be accepted by a sizeable proportion.

By contrast, up to two fifths (44%) of theatergoers do not feel that they understand why booking and restoration fees are charged. Why must each ticket have a booking fee? What is that money actually paying for? And why have a transaction fee on top of this?

Just over half would prefer such fees to be 'inside' the price paid i.e. not expressed separately 'on top' of the face value of the ticket, so the customer would be presented with a simple price for the ticket which includes any fees. Whilst this might not lower the actual money paid for a ticket, it would potentially lessen the annoyance of being reminded of such fees. (Paradoxically, ending the practice of expressing fees separately from the 'face value' of a ticket would almost certainly be detrimental to customers' interests since unscrupulous tickets sellers could then more easily – i.e. less noticeably - increase their fees.)

Assuming, then, that ticketing fees are unlikely to go away, the challenge for theatres and ticket agents is to better explain and justify the reasons for such fees. Such justifications usually focus on the convenience to the customer (e.g. telephone and web booking) that such things as computerized ticketing systems, centralized box offices and relationships with third party ticket agents have brought. Ticket-selling functionalities (whether within a theatre organization or as separate ticket agents) have evolved to be paid for (usually) by 'outside' ticketing fees. Putting the case for ticketing fees is a complex and difficult argument to make to customers, particularly now that the days when buying a ticket usually meant a trip in person to a box office are a distant memory for the older theatergoer, and completely alien to the young.

Finally, and slightly more positively: whilst more than half of respondents said the presence and size of booking fees influences their buying decision (presumably, negatively), this was not an overwhelming majority. Shopping around for lower fees is no bad thing for the operation of the market. And, as recent record attendance figures would suggest, customers eventually seem to grit their teeth and buy their tickets.

8 TICKETING
SERVICES

BOX O

LIKELIHOOD TO USE NEW TICKETING SERVICES

Theatregoers completing the online survey were asked about how likely they would be to use certain new ways of buying or collecting tickets if these services were more widely available:

- Paying for a theatre ticket via one's mobile phone – a ticket is booked with a ticketing website the cost being added to one's mobile phone bill.

- Receiving one's ticket as a barcode or unique reference number on one's mobile phone which is then scanned/checked at the theatre.

- Receiving one's ticket as an email which is printed at home/work by the theatregoer and scanned at the theatre.

- Buying one's ticket at the theatre using an electronic kiosk – like those in use at many cinemas.

The most popular service was that of the email ticket which could be printed at home/work before going to the theatre. Eighty eight per cent said they would be certain to or likely to do this if the service was available. Thirty one per cent would be certain to use this method if available.

Buying a ticket at an electronic kiosk was also well received. Two in three would be either certain or likely to do this if the option was there (one assumes attitudes towards electronic kiosks encompass collection of pre-paid tickets as well as purchase of tickets).

There are now some new ways you can pay for and receive theatre tickets. How likely, if at all, would you be to use each of the following ticketing services if they were widely/easily available?

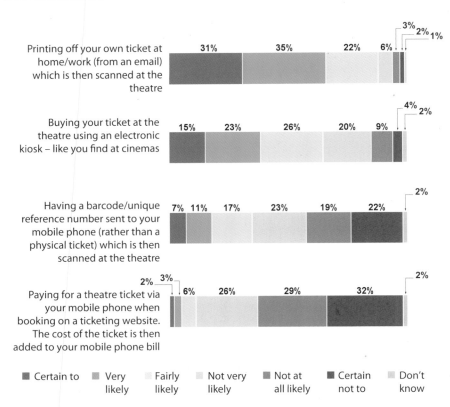

Base: All online survey respondents (716)

Source: Ipsos MORI

- Those who tend to purchase theatre tickets 1-7 days before a performance and those aged 16-34 are the most positive towards kiosks with 78% and 71% respectively being certain or likely to use them.

- A third of theatregoers in the online survey (34% certain or likely to use this) would be happy to have a barcode or a unique reference number sent to a mobile phone instead of a physical ticket.

- Again, those who tend to purchase theatre tickets 1 – 7 days in advance, and younger theatregoers (16-34) would be more willing to use this service (48% and 58% are certain or likely to use).

- Purchase of tickets via a mobile phone was by some way the least popular of the four options with just one in ten (11%) certain or likely to use this service. A third (32%) would be certain not to use this service.

- Younger people are again more positive towards this idea - 17% would be certain or likely to use this service; 45% of those aged over 55 would be certain not to use the service.

- Those who visit the theatre most often are also cautious about this idea – amongst those making 6 or more visits to London theatre in the last year 38% would be certain not to use this service.

LIKELIHOOD TO USE NEW METHODS TO BOOK THEATRE TICKETS AT THE LAST MINUTE

Nearly all theatregoers (91%) would be willing to book theatre tickets at the last minute online.

Eighty four per cent would be certain or likely to book tickets at the last minute over the phone.

Using a mobile phone to book tickets over the internet was the option least positively received. Just 21% would be certain or likely to use this method.

- Those aged 16-34 are more likely to say that they would try this, with 34% stating they are certain or fairly likely to. This further illustrates younger theatregoers' openness to trying different technological approaches.

How likely, if at all, would you be to use each of the following methods, if they were available, to book theatre tickets at the last minute (i.e. the day of the performance or a few days before the performance)?

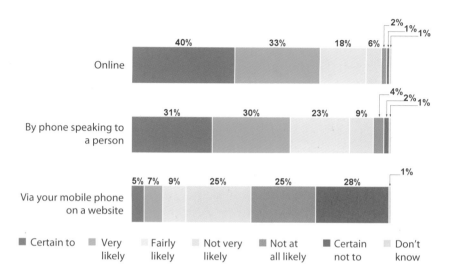

Online: 40% 33% 18% 6% 2% 1% 1%

By phone speaking to a person: 31% 30% 23% 9% 4% 2% 1%

Via your mobile phone on a website: 5% 7% 9% 25% 25% 28% 1%

Certain to / Very likely / Fairly likely / Not very likely / Not at all likely / Certain not to / Don't know

Base: All online survey respondents (716)

Source: Ipsos MORI

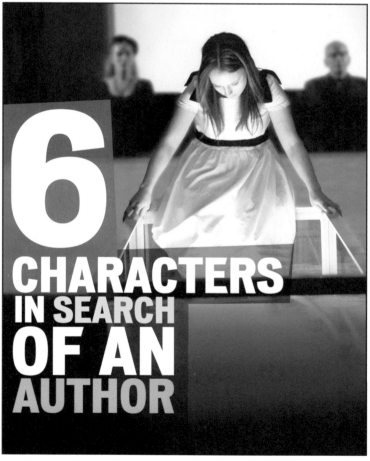

A production by Headlong Theatre presented in the West End by MJE productions

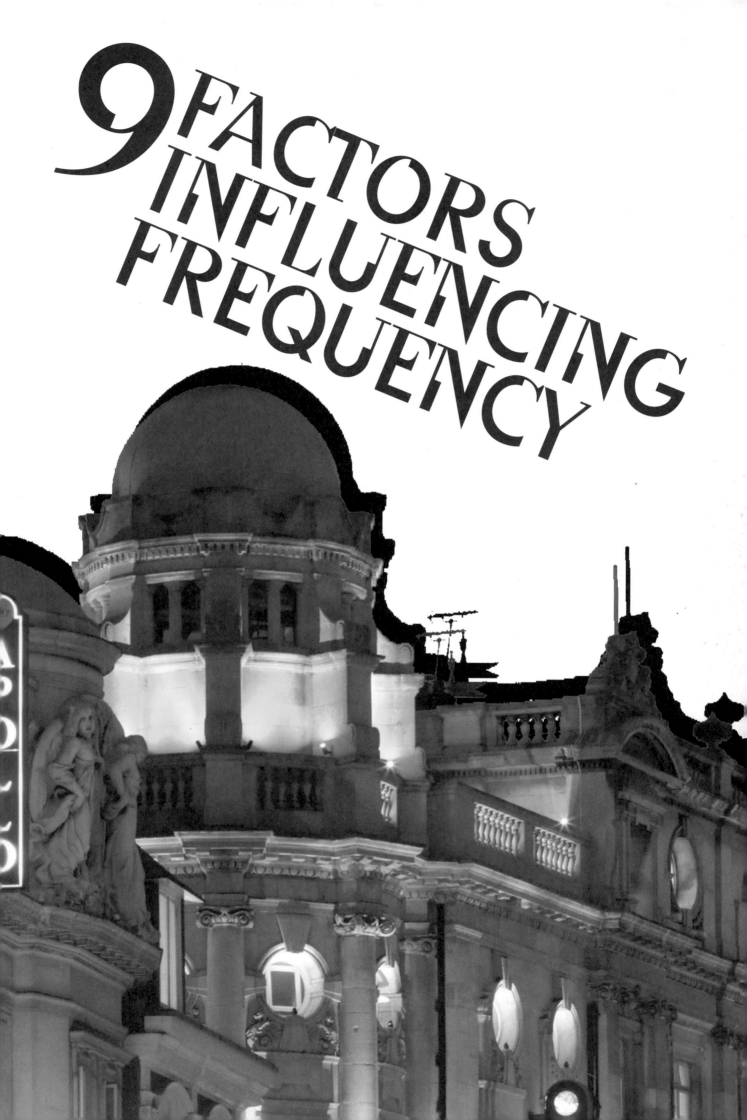

9 FACTORS INFLUENCING FREQUENCY

WHAT PREVENTS PEOPLE FROM VISITING THE THEATRE MORE OFTEN?

When asked about factors that prevent them from visiting the theatre, audience members mention a range of factors. Seven in ten (69%) state that cost stops them visiting the theatre more often. Half (52%) state it is the price of tickets themselves, while a further third (32%) say it is too expensive generally and a quarter (23%) just do not have enough time/ are too busy. Other influential factors include booking fees and ticket availability.

Factors unrelated to cost such as the show finishing too late (5%), the choice of shows (5%) and a lack of information about shows (5%) are mentioned by small but significant proportions of visitors.

There is also a small group of theatregoers (14%) who state that they already visit the theatre as much as they would like.

Issues of cost are clearly a barrier to visiting the theatre, but which groups does it affect particularly?

- Seven in ten female theatregoers (73%) are stopped from visiting the theatre more often by cost reasons.

- Seventy seven per cent of theatregoers aged 16-24 find cost a barrier. This is compared to 69% of those aged 35-54 and 64% of those aged 55+.

If you would like to visit the theatre more often than you do, what, if anything, stops you from doing so?

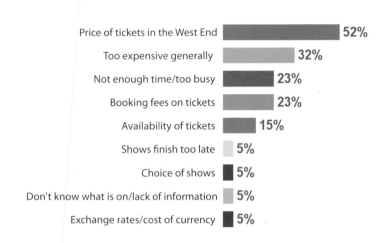

Base: All answering (4264)　　　　　　　　　　　　　Source: Ipsos MORI

- Around half (47%) of those purchasing their ticket on the day of the performance refer to ticket prices being too expensive and a third (35%) that visiting the theatre is too expensive generally. This may offer an explanation for last-minute ticket purchasing in order to obtain discounts.

- Nearly three in ten (27%) of those aged 55+ are put off by booking fees on tickets, more so than any other age group.

- Around half of those visiting with one other person (54%), state that ticket price is a barrier. This can perhaps be attributed to the fact that sizeable numbers of these are visiting with a partner, family, children or friends.

- Nearly three in ten male theatregoers (27%) state that they do not have enough time/are too busy.

IF YOU WOULD LIKE TO VISIT THE THEATRE MORE OFTEN THAN YOU DO, WHAT, IF ANYTHING, STOPS YOU FROM DOING SO?

	Gender %		Age %				Origin %			*Performance Type %				Income %			Working Status %	
	M	F	16-24	25-34	35-54	55+	London	Rest of UK	Overseas	M	P	O	D	Up to £20,000	£20,001 - £50,000	£50,001+	Working	Not Working
Base	1368	2591	522	774	1333	1271	1801	1711	676	2140	978	771	324	1244	1518	732	2684	1247
Nothing, I already visit as much as I would like	19	12	9	11	13	22	14	13	18	12	17	27	15	11	14	20	13	17
Price of tickets in the West End	44	56	56	55	50	51	61	54	26	53	50	46	55	56	54	35	52	51
Too expensive generally	28	33	40	32	29	29	31	31	34	32	28	26	37	41	28	21	30	35
Not enough time/too busy	27	21	28	29	24	16	23	21	27	22	25	23	22	19	26	31	26	17
Booking fees on tickets	23	23	17	21	24	27	28	24	9	23	24	22	24	25	23	20	24	21
Availability of tickets	14	15	14	15	16	12	16	15	12	13	18	18	21	13	14	20	16	12
Shows finish too late	4	6	3	5	5	5	3	8	2	5	4	8	7	4	6	4	5	4
Choice of shows	6	4	4	5	4	6	5	4	6	4	8	6	4	4	5	7	4	6
Don't know what is on/lack of information about shows	5	4	6	7	3	3	5	5	3	4	6	3	6	5	4	5	5	4
Exchange rates/ cost of currency	4	4	9	3	4	4	*	*	24	5	6	1	2	4	3	5	3	7
Any	**81**	**88**	**91**	**89**	**87**	**78**	**86**	**87**	**82**	**88**	**83**	**73**	**85**	**89**	**86**	**80**	**87**	**83**
Cost	61	73	77	72	69	64	72	70	60	72	64	58	72	78	69	53	69	71

*Performance Type key:
M = Musical
P = Play
O = Opera
D = Dance
NB: Entertainment type performances are not reported here due to the small base size

FACTORS PUTTING THEATREGOERS OFF VISITING CENTRAL LONDON

Around half (52%) of theatregoers state that the associated costs of visiting central London can put them off visiting the theatre. Issues relating to public transport ceasing too early (14%) and their personal safety (9%) are also of importance, but cost is by far the most mentioned reason.

One in ten (10%) cite the congestion charge as an off-putting factor, while a further 14% mention problems with parking and 8% traffic congestion.

In addition, others mention crime (7%), begging (6%) or cleanliness (4%).

The response options for this question have been updated since the 2003 survey, particularly the option 'too expensive generally' which was not included and this seems to have impacted on all answers relating to cost. Where direct comparisons can be made, we have seen a drop in the number of mentions for public transport finishing too early (22% versus 14% now), begging (16% down to 6%) and crime (15% falling to 7%).

Certain groups are more likely to mention reasons around cost and expense of visiting the theatre.

- As would be expected, around half of those earning up to £20,000 per annum (52%), and between £20,001-£35,000 (48%) state that it is too expensive generally.

Some people have said that the factors below can put them off visiting the theatre in central London. Which, if any, applies to you?

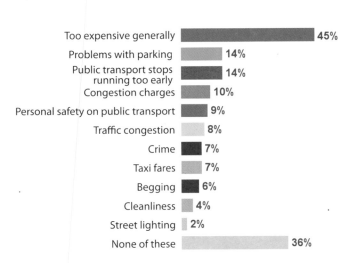

	2008 (%)	2003 (%)
Too expensive generally	45	N/A
Problems with parking	14	N/A
Public transport stops running too early	14	22
Congestion charges	10	13
Personal safety on public transport	9	17
Traffic congestion	8	14
Crime	7	15
Taxi fares	7	12
Begging	6	16
Cleanliness	4	14
Street lighting	2	5
None of these	36	44

Base: All answering: (2008: 3960, 2003: 6209)

Source: Ipsos MORI

- As previously mentioned, theatregoers attending productions including opera, dance and plays tend to be more affluent, so cost is not as much an issue. Two fifths (41%) of those attending an opera say that cost is an off-putting factor, this compares to over half (55%) of those attending a musical.

- Working status, interestingly, has little impact on what factors may put theatregoers off visiting.

  - However, when considering ethnicity, six in ten (60%) of non-white theatregoers state cost as an off-putting factor compared to 51% of white theatregoers.

- Those attending in a party of two (47%), three in four people (45%) and 5+ (47%) say it is too expensive generally.

- As would be expected, over half of theatregoers aged under 25 (55%) say it is too expensive generally, with this dropping to 40% for those aged 55+.

- Issues around transport in central London are important to different groups, for example a sixth of those aged 34 and under (16%) state that public transport stops too early, whereas a similar number of those aged 35+ (15%) state problems with parking as a factor that can put them off visiting the theatre in central London.

- Overseas visitors, in particular those from North America, consistently perceive fewer factors as off-putting than theatregoers from the UK.

SOME PEOPLE HAVE SAID THAT THE FACTORS BELOW CAN PUT THEM OFF VISITING THE THEATRE IN CENTRAL LONDON. WHICH, IF ANY, APPLIES TO YOU PERSONALLY?

	Gender %		Age %				Origin %			*Performance Type %				Income %			Working Status %	
	M	F	16-24	25-34	35-54	55+	London	Rest of UK	Overseas	M	P	O	D	Up to £20,000	£20,001 - £50,000	£50,001+	Working	Not Working
Base	1306	2473	507	726	1280	1210	1641	1588	656	2009	881	718	307	1190	1449	691	2557	1191
Too expensive generally	40	48	55	48	44	40	45	48	40	48	40	34	43	52	44	35	45	47
Problems with parking	16	13	14	11	15	15	14	18	5	15	12	12	13	14	13	15	14	15
Public transport stops running too early	13	14	16	16	12	12	14	15	9	13	15	12	18	16	14	9	14	13
Congestion charges	11	9	9	9	10	9	9	13	4	11	7	9	8	10	8	9	10	9
Personal safety on public transport	7	11	9	7	10	10	9	11	7	10	8	10	9	10	10	6	9	10
Traffic congestion	10	8	9	7	8	10	7	11	7	9	6	7	7	11	7	6	8	9
Crime	7	7	8	6	7	7	6	8	6	8	6	5	4	8	6	6	7	7
Taxi fares	7	6	8	6	6	6	7	7	5	7	6	6	5	6	6	8	6	7
Begging	6	5	6	4	6	6	5	8	4	6	4	7	5	6	5	6	6	5
Cleanliness	5	4	2	3	5	6	4	5	2	4	3	7	3	3	5	4	5	3
Street lighting	2	2	2	2	1	2	2	2	2	2	2	2	1	2	1	1	2	2
None	36	34	26	34	37	42	37	30	47	33	43	45	39	29	37	48	36	35
At least one	64	66	74	66	63	58	63	70	53	67	57	55	62	71	63	52	64	65
Cost	52	54	61	54	50	45	51	56	42	55	45	41	49	58	50	42	51	53
Public Transport	20	21	22	21	20	19	20	23	15	20	21	19	23	22	21	13	20	20

*Performance Type key:
M = Musical
P = Play
O = Opera
D = Dance
NB: Entertainment type performances are not reported here due to the small base size

10 MOTIVATIONS FOR VISITING THEATRE

WHY DO YOU VISIT THE THEATRE?

The online survey asked theatregoers taking part about why they visited the theatre generally. The desire to be entertained is the most popular reason – nine in ten (90%) theatregoers taking part in the online questionnaire mention this.

The reputation of the show (66%), personal recommendations (49%) and special offers/promotions (47%) are also key motivations.

- For those taking part in the online questionnaire personal recommendations are influential for those who tend to book tickets over the telephone (62%).

- Just under half of theatregoers said that good reviews in the media encourage them to attend shows.

- Two in five theatregoers completing the online survey find the theatre a good way to have a night out with friends (38%). This is a more influential reason for women (43%) than men (28%). A night out with friends is also more appealing to younger people (49% of those aged 16-34).

- Price, promotions and special offers are mentioned by just under half (47%) – and is a particularly influential factor with younger people (55% of 16-34 year olds).

- A third (33%) of theatregoers in the online survey mention the writer or composer of a show as a reason for visiting, this is particularly the case for men (42% compared with 28% women). This also motivates those in the older age group with 47% of over 55s mentioning the writer or composer.

For which, if any, of the following reasons do you visit the theatre?

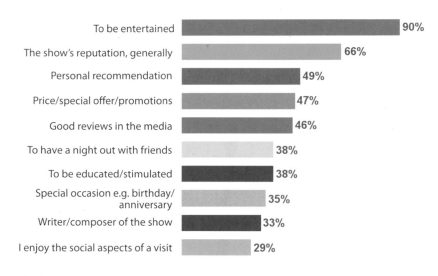

To be entertained	90%
The show's reputation, generally	66%
Personal recommendation	49%
Price/special offer/promotions	47%
Good reviews in the media	46%
To have a night out with friends	38%
To be educated/stimulated	38%
Special occasion e.g. birthday/anniversary	35%
Writer/composer of the show	33%
I enjoy the social aspects of a visit	29%

Base: All online survey respondents (716)   Source: Ipsos MORI

La Cage aux Folles

ASSOCIATIONS WITH WEST END THEATRE

Theatregoers who took part in the online survey were asked their opinion about a number of statements relating to West End theatre, the West End and London itself.

- Seven in ten (70%) theatregoers strongly agree that West End theatre forms an important part of London's culture.

- Three in five (58%) strongly agree that theatres help make the West End a vibrant place.

- Fifty four per cent of theatregoers completing the online survey feel strongly that West End theatre makes a vital contribution to London tourism.

- Almost two in three (58%) theatregoers agree that visiting West End theatre is an important part of their life.

- The statement which sees the highest levels of disagreement is 'visiting West End theatre represents good value for money'. In contrast to the other propositions where there was fairly substantial agreement, 37% agree with the statement and looking at those who strongly agree this falls to just 6%. A quarter (25%) of theatregoers taking part in the online survey tend to disagree with the statement and 5% are strongly opposed to it.

The following statements relate to West End theatre. To what extent do you agree, or disagree, with each?

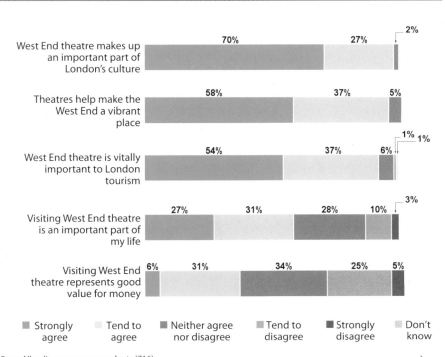

Base: All online survey respondents (716)

Source: Ipsos MORI

WHICH SHOW TO SEE? INFLUENCES ON THEATREGOERS

The general reputation of the show has the most impact on audience members when deciding on what show to see - mentioned by 57% of all theatregoers. General reputation is difficult to define, but is presumably an amalgam of many of the other factors in this question e.g. word of mouth reviews, creative team or cast, awards won plus, for revivals, previous productions.

Personal recommendation is the next most mentioned reason (37%). The influence of personal recommendation is something that we see consistently with audiences at other cultural activities such as museum and gallery visitors. Word of mouth remains important though the means of transmission might be changing in this age of email, Facebook and Twitter.

Positive reviews of the performance in the media (35%) completes the top three influences on deciding which show to attend.

This mirrors the results from 2003 where these were also the top three most influential factors mentioned.

The price of the ticket or a special offer or promotion is mentioned by one in five audience members (21%) as a reason for attending the show.

Additionally, the proportion of theatregoers stating price/special offer/promotion, has increased by three percentage points since the last theatre audience survey. Whilst still fairly small, it is the largest increase for any of the factors for this question – perhaps evidence of people thinking more carefully about how they spend their money.

Which, if any, of these factors influenced you to watch this particular production today?

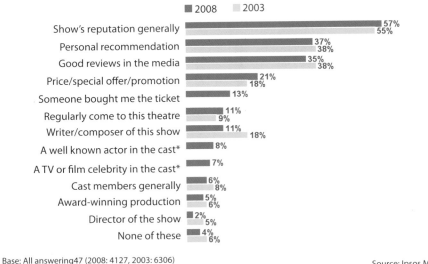

Base: All answering47 (2008: 4127, 2003: 6306)
* In 2003, a single factor – A 'Star' in the cast – scored an 8% response

Source: Ipsos MORI

Factors relating to the cast and the show itself are important to some audience members - 11% mention the writer or composer of the show, 8% mention a well-known actor appearing, 7% a TV or film celebrity in the cast, and 6% 'cast members generally'.

The fact that 'writer/composer of the show' is ranked as a more important factor than the presence of a well-known actor or TV/film celebrity in the cast will be welcomed by some for whom 'the play's the thing' but would seem to run counter to the views of many that 'event theatre' with 'star casting' has grown ever more important in recent years. It cannot be discounted, however, that the presence of three separate options on casting in this survey (a well-known actor, a TV or film celebrity and cast members generally) might have reduced the number of theatregoers choosing each individual option and all three responses could be considered when gauging the true importance of casting.

The rating for 'writer/composer of the show' fell from 18% in 2003 to 11% in 2008. This might reflect other factors becoming more important and/or a lessening in the prominence of writers in West End productions (e.g. fewer recent musicals from 'name' writers or more juke-box or film adaptation musicals with relatively anonymous creative teams).

- The general reputation of the show is particularly important to the youngest visitors (62% of 16-24 year olds). This is also true of North American visitors (66%), those seeing a musical (62%) and also those seeing a matinee (72%). Theatregoers for whom the theatre was the main reason for visiting London are also influenced by this (63%).

- Women (38%), the youngest audience members (16-24 year olds – 52%), North American visitors (44%), those buying their ticket on the day of the performance (42%)

Wicked: Brinkhoff/Mögenburg

and those seeing a musical (43%) are those more likely to be influenced by personal recommendations.

- Good reviews in the press were particularly influential amongst UK visitors (36%), but this would be expected given a greater access to UK media. Interestingly, they are also more important to North American visitors (39%) than other overseas visitors. This may reflect the fact that many shows (particularly musicals) appear in very similar productions in both London and New York (and touring across the USA), so a US press review might have influenced a London theatre visit.

- UK theatregoers from outside London are influenced by some element of the 'cast' (either a particular actor or the cast generally - 20%), as are those visiting the theatre alone (24%) and those attending a play (22%), this compares to 17% of all theatregoers.

- Looking particularly at the influence of a well known actor in the cast – UK based visitors (9%), particularly those from outside London (10%) are more influenced by this, as are those who visit the theatre most frequently (12% amongst those who have been to the theatre 6 or more times in the last 12 months). Audience members seeing a play are more likely to be swayed by a well known actor (12%) as are those for whom the theatre was the main reason for their visit to London (11%).

- A TV or film celebrity in the cast is particularly persuasive for certain groups – women (9%), again UK visitors (9%), particularly those from outside London (10%), theatregoers who are working (8%), frequent theatre visitors (9%), those for whom the theatre was their main reason for visiting London (10%), those seeing a musical (9%) and those seeing a production at a small theatre (13%).

- One in ten audience members are regular 'attenders' at a particular theatre (11%) and so this plays a part in influencing their visit. 'Venue-loyalty' such as this is far more common in the subsidised London theatres (e.g. Royal Opera House, Coliseum, National Theatre) than in the commercial West End.

WHICH, IF ANY, OF THESE FACTORS INFLUENCED YOU TO WATCH THIS PARTICULAR PRODUCTION TODAY?

	Gender %		Age %				Origin %			*Performance Type %				Income %			Working Status %	
	M	F	16-24	25-34	35-54	55+	London	Rest of UK	Overseas	M	P	O	D	Up to £20,000	£20,001 - £50,000	£50,001+	Working	Not Working
Base	1387	2610	518	775	1347	1302	1714	1638	699	2069	933	753	320	1231	1528	730	2709	1261
The show's reputation, generally	58	56	62	55	57	54	51	60	59	62	44	38	56	55	58	56	57	56
Personal recommendation	34	38	52	40	34	30	37	36	41	43	27	16	17	40	37	34	37	38
Good reviews in the media	36	34	34	30	35	38	33	38	30	36	41	22	14	33	34	39	34	37
Price/special offer/promotion	18	22	20	25	22	17	25	19	14	21	18	14	18	23	22	15	22	18
Someone bought me the ticket	11	14	21	15	11	9	16	11	10	12	13	11	17	17	11	10	12	15
Regularly come to this theatre	14	10	7	8	9	20	17	9	5	4	19	54	29	10	10	15	10	15
Writer/composer of this show	13	10	8	7	10	17	12	9	13	7	15	41	16	9	10	15	10	15
A well known actor in the cast	7	9	7	7	8	9	8	10	4	8	12	6	3	8	9	9	8	9
A TV or film celebrity in the cast	5	9	7	9	9	5	7	10	3	9	9	1	1	8	8	5	8	6
Cast members generally	7	6	5	7	5	7	9	6	3	4	10	10	11	6	6	7	6	7
Award-winning production	6	4	7	3	5	4	4	4	8	5	5	1	1	5	4	6	4	7
Director of this show	2	2	2	2	1	3	3	2	1	1	5	5	2	2	2	2	2	3
None	4	4	3	4	4	3	3	4	5	4	4	3	5	4	4	3	4	3
At least one	96	96	97	96	96	97	97	96	95	96	96	97	95	96	96	97	96	97
Reputation/ Reviews/ Recommendation	79	79	84	78	79	77	75	81	84	84	72	55	68	78	80	78	79	78
Writer/Composer/ Director	**13**	**11**	**10**	**8**	**11**	**18**	**14**	**9**	**14**	**8**	**18**	**42**	**16**	**10**	**11**	**16**	**10**	**16**
Cast members	**15**	**18**	**15**	**16**	**17**	**18**	**18**	**20**	**8**	**17**	**22**	**15**	**13**	**18**	**18**	**16**	**17**	**17**

*Performance Type key: M = Musical   P = Play   O = Opera   D = Dance

NB: Entertainment type performances are not reported here due to the small base size

REALITY TV SHOWS AND ATTENDANCE

In the online questionnaire, the influence of reality television on attendance at the theatre was measured.

Forty per cent state they have regularly watched a theatre-themed reality TV programme – increasing to 56% among those attending a musical. Around a quarter have watched recent programmes based on the casting of lead roles in Joseph ('Any Dream Will Do') (29%), The Sound of Music ('How Do You Solve A Problem Like Maria') (29%) or Oliver! ('I'd Do Anything') (25%), whilst 11% had watched the 'Grease' casting show 'Grease is the Word'.

Female theatregoers as well as middle-aged visitors (35-54 year olds) were more likely to watch theatre–themed TV shows (respectively 45% and 48%).

In all, 40% of online theatregoers had watched at least one of the four TV shows.

Have you regularly watched any of the following theatre-themed reality TV shows?

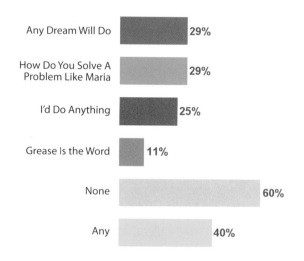

Base: All online survey respondents (716)

Source: Ipsos MORI

Theatre-related TV shows encouraged a third (34%) of theatregoers who watched them regularly to attend West End musicals in general.

Around half (47%) agree that watching a theatre-based reality TV show makes them more likely to attend the musical featured in the TV show.

• This is also particularly the case for younger theatregoers compared to older theatregoers (51% of those aged 16-34 versus 33% of those 55+).

A fifth of those who watch theatre-related reality TV shows agree that watching the show has made them more likely to attend other non-musical productions in the West End. A similar proportion agrees that watching these programmes has made them more likely to attend productions outside London's West End.

This suggests that for certain people theatre-related reality TV shows can be influential in promoting visits to the theatre for the TV-featured production itself (which one would expect), for musicals in general, and – for a small proportion – to non-musical performances and productions outside the West End.

To what extent do you agree or disagree with the following statements regarding theatre-based reality TV shows?

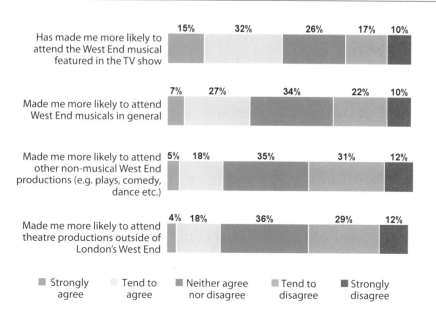

Base: All respondents who watched any theatre-based reality TV show (285)

Source: Ipsos MORI

11 MARKETING AND COMMUNICATION

Photographer: Carl O'Connell

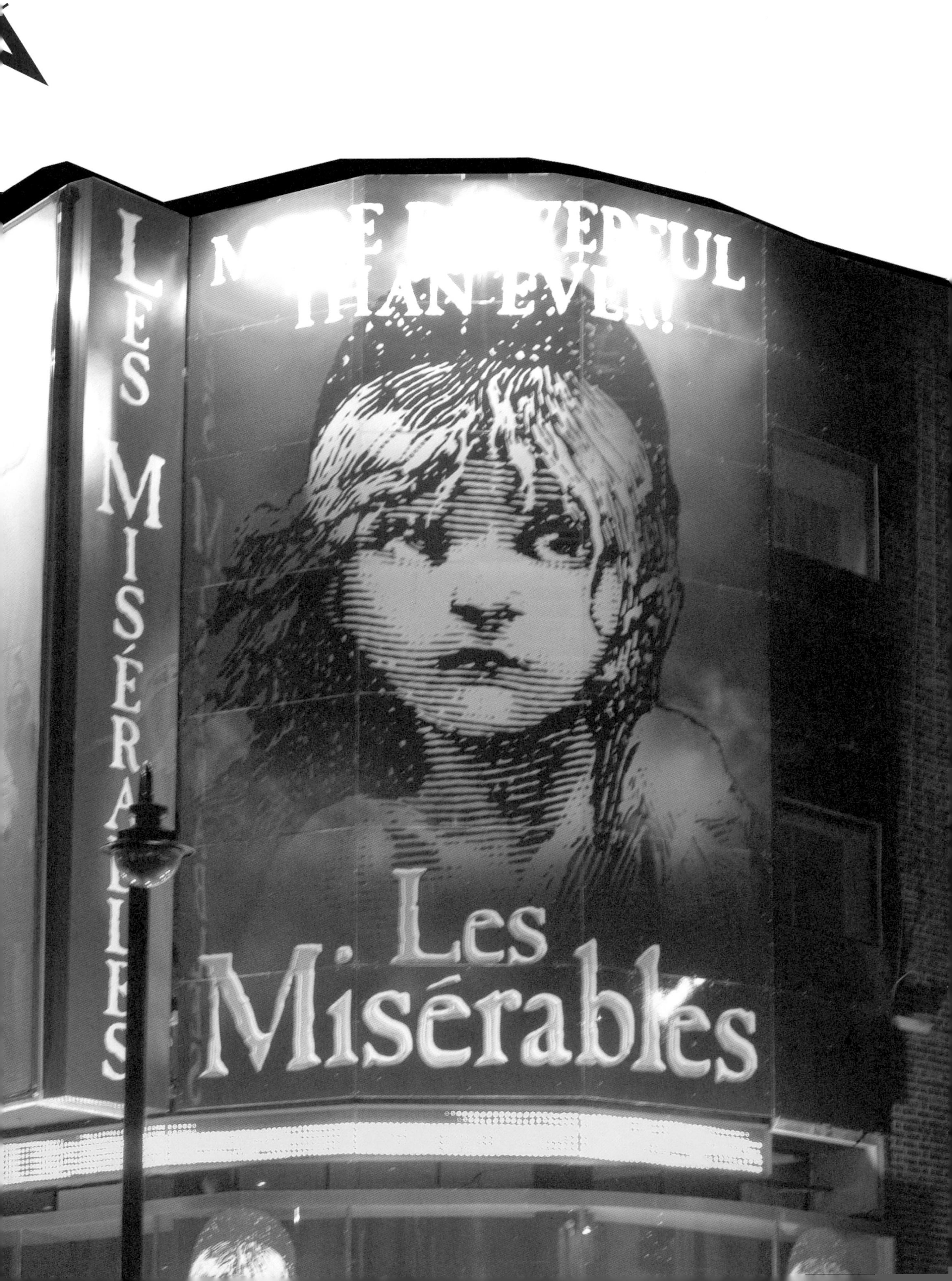
Les Misérables

GATHERING INFORMATION ABOUT THIS PERFORMANCE

Closely linked to influencing factors are the places and ways that people discover information about performances.

When asked about finding information about the performance they attended, word of mouth is the most popular information source (53%). This reflects the power of personal recommendations in deciding on which performance to see which continues the trend from previous theatre audience surveys - 2003 (55%) and 1997 (39%).

Word of mouth is followed by press coverage – whether that is advertising, reviews or features (23%), which in turn is closely followed by websites (22%). It is worth noting that the proportion of theatregoers mentioning a website is up from just 11% in 2003 (websites were not asked about in 1997).

What's on listings, which provide information about many performances, are mentioned by 15% of audience members, although this has seen a fall since 2003, where one in five audience members mentioned this source (21%). It is possible that the internet has replaced what's on listings for finding much information.

A performance is not necessarily a one-off experience for all theatregoers – 15% of audience members are returning to a production they have already seen before, just marginally higher than the proportion in 2003 and 1997 (both 13%).

Advertising, reviews or features on television are sources of information for 13% of theatregoers, this increasing

How did you hear about this production?

Top mentions

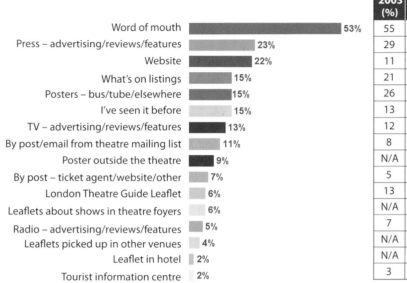

	2003 (%)	1997 (%)
Word of mouth — 53%	55	39
Press – advertising/reviews/features — 23%	29	55
Website — 22%	11	N/A
What's on listings — 15%	21	N/A
Posters – bus/tube/elsewhere — 15%	26	13
I've seen it before — 15%	13	13
TV – advertising/reviews/features — 13%	12	10
By post/email from theatre mailing list — 11%	8	7
Poster outside the theatre — 9%	N/A	N/A
By post – ticket agent/website/other — 7%	5	N/A
London Theatre Guide Leaflet — 6%	13	9
Leaflets about shows in theatre foyers — 6%	N/A	N/A
Radio – advertising/reviews/features — 5%	7	6
Leaflets picked up in other venues — 4%	N/A	N/A
Leaflet in hotel — 2%	N/A	N/A
Tourist information centre — 2%	3	N/A

Base: All answering (2008: 4146, 2003: 6240, 1997: 6880)   Source: Ipsos MORI

to 17% of those attending a musical. Coverage on the radio, by contrast, is only mentioned by 5% of theatregoers.

Six percent of audience members found information about the performance in the London Theatre Guide, published by the Society of London Theatre. This is a marked fall from 2003 where 13% of audience members had used the Guide, and is now back in line with 1997 (9%).

• Overseas visitors are more likely than UK based visitors to use the London Theatre Guide (11% of overseas visitors compared to 5% of UK visitors and 3% of London visitors).

• The rise of the internet for discovering information is likely to have had an impact on this – particularly as the London Theatre Guide is now available online (www.

officiallondontheatre.co.uk) so some theatregoers may have switched to using the Guide in this way.

• Those aged under 35 are more likely to be influenced by word of mouth (71% for 16-24 year olds and 60% for 25-34 year olds).

  - Those visiting the theatre in larger groups (5 or more) are also more influenced by word of mouth (65%).

• Press coverage has more impact with audience members aged 55 and over (27%), as it does with UK visitors (26%), although this is to be expected given that the UK press is more likely to have coverage of London shows.

Aida. Photographer: Tristram Kenton

- Those for whom visiting the theatre was the main reason for visiting London are also influenced by press reviews (26%) suggesting that this is an important source of information to those not living in London.

- Websites are influential among those aged both 25-34 (26%) and 35-54 (24%). They are also used by overseas visitors (25% of all overseas visitors and this rises to 32% amongst European visitors) which is logical given the fact they may not be in London long prior to the show they see and so may 'research' the show online prior to their visit.

- Websites are used by a larger proportion of audience members at an opera (27%) and also at dance performances (31%).

- Those visiting alone are more likely to have used 'what's on listings' (19%).

- Television coverage and theatre mailing lists (whether post or email) are more likely to be mentioned by UK based visitors (14% and 13% respectively). Visitors aged over 55 are more likely to mention mailing lists (16%).

- When sources of information are grouped together, audience members aged over 35 are more likely to mention information in the media generally (34%), whereas those aged under 35 make more mention of posters and leaflets.

  - 37% of 16-24 year olds mention posters.

  - 31% of 25-34 year olds mention posters.

  - 17% of under 25s mention leaflets.

HOW DID YOU HEAR ABOUT THIS PRODUCTION?

	Gender %		Age %				Origin %			*Performance Type %				Income %			Working Status %	
	M	F	16-24	25-34	35-54	55+	London	Rest of UK	Overseas	M	P	O	D	Up to £20,000	£20,001 - £50,000	£50,001+	Working	Not Working
Base	1390	2606	524	781	1338	1298	1725	1646	703	2070	934	764	324	1234	1522	729	2705	1260
Word of mouth	51	54	71	60	50	41	54	52	53	59	45	27	35	55	54	49	54	52
Press – advertising/reviews/features	25	23	19	20	25	27	25	26	13	24	28	18	10	22	24	26	23	24
Website	23	21	24	26	24	15	22	20	25	21	20	27	31	21	22	23	24	17
'What's on' listings (eg in newspaper/website)	15	14	14	13	14	17	15	15	13	14	18	9	14	14	14	16	14	16
Posters – bus/tube/elsewhere	12	16	30	24	10	4	18	11	16	17	10	4	10	17	14	12	15	15
I've seen it before	14	14	14	13	15	15	14	16	13	17	6	18	16	14	15	11	14	15
Television – advertising/reviews/features	9	14	14	13	14	11	11	17	7	17	5	2	1	15	14	7	13	12
By post/email from theatre mailing list	13	10	7	8	9	16	17	9	3	6	15	49	24	9	11	14	10	13
Poster outside the theatre	9	9	18	12	7	4	11	6	11	9	11	4	7	10	9	7	8	10
By post/email from ticket agent/website/other	6	7	8	9	6	4	8	7	3	7	6	5	7	8	6	7	7	5
The 'London Theatre Guide' leaflet	6	6	11	5	5	6	3	6	11	7	5	2	2	8	5	5	6	7
Leaflets about shows in theatre foyers	5	6	10	5	5	4	7	5	4	6	5	5	6	7	5	5	5	6
Radio – advertising/reviews/features	5	6	6	5	6	5	6	6	2	6	5	3	2	5	6	4	6	5
Leaflets picked up in other venues (eg café, shop, library)	4	4	8	5	3	3	4	4	4	5	2	2	4	5	3	3	4	5
Leaflet in hotel	2	2	4	2	2	1	1	1	6	3	1	*	1	3	2	2	2	2
Tourist information centre	3	2	5	2	1	1	1	1	6	2	1	1	1	2	1	2	1	3
Leaflets	9	10	17	9	9	7	10	8	12	11	7	7	10	12	8	8	9	11
By post/email	17	15	11	14	14	19	22	14	5	10	19	51	29	14	16	19	15	16
Posters	17	20	37	31	14	7	25	14	21	21	18	7	16	21	19	16	19	20
Media	30	33	28	29	34	34	32	38	18	35	31	20	11	32	33	30	32	32

*Performance Type key: M = Musical   P = Play   O = Opera   D = Dance

NB: Entertainment type performances are not reported here due to the small base size

Les Miserables

GATHERING INFORMATION ABOUT THEATRE-GOING GENERALLY

Word of mouth is also the most mentioned source of information when asking about going to the theatre generally (65%), reinforcing the message that we have consistently seen that word of mouth and personal recommendations hold a definite sway over deciding to visit the theatre. This has increased noticeably since 2003 when it was mentioned by 36% of theatregoers.

Press coverage follows this (48%) and then 'what's on listings' (33%). 'What's on listings' receive a much higher level of mentions as a source of general information than as a source of information relating to a specific production, suggesting that theatregoers may use listings to gain an idea of what is showing, but go on to use other methods to research a particular production.

Websites are mentioned by 33% of theatregoers as a general source of information. This has increased from 17% in 2003 (this question was not asked in 1997).

The 'London Theatre Guide' leaflet is mentioned by 13% as a general source of information.

Generally, which, if any, other sources of information are effective in encouraging you to go to the theatre?

Top mentions

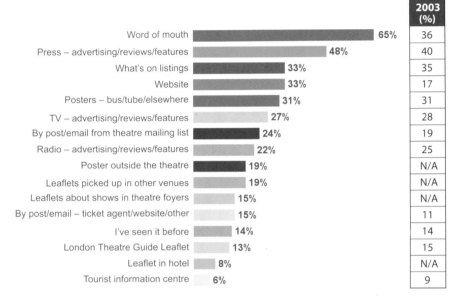

		2003 (%)
Word of mouth	65%	36
Press – advertising/reviews/features	48%	40
What's on listings	33%	35
Website	33%	17
Posters – bus/tube/elsewhere	31%	31
TV – advertising/reviews/features	27%	28
By post/email from theatre mailing list	24%	19
Radio – advertising/reviews/features	22%	25
Poster outside the theatre	19%	N/A
Leaflets picked up in other venues	19%	N/A
Leaflets about shows in theatre foyers	15%	N/A
By post/email – ticket agent/website/other	15%	11
I've seen it before	14%	14
London Theatre Guide Leaflet	13%	15
Leaflet in hotel	8%	N/A
Tourist information centre	6%	9

Base: All answering (2008: 3611, 2003: 4246)

Source: Ipsos MORI

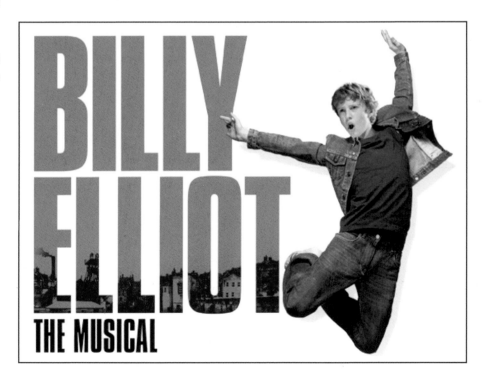

AND GENERALLY, WHICH, IF ANY, OTHER SOURCES OF INFORMATION ARE EFFECTIVE IN ENCOURAGING YOU TO GO TO THE THEATRE?

	Gender %		Age %				Origin %			*Performance Type %				Income %			Working Status %	
	M	F	16-24	25-34	35-54	55+	London	Rest of UK	Overseas	M	P	O	D	Up to £20,000	£20,001-£50,000	£50,001+	Working	Not Working
Base	1210	2295	473	698	1155	1134	1540	1433	583	1762	834	681	290	1080	1349	632	2361	1116
Word of mouth	63	67	69	71	68	56	70	63	63	65	70	54	59	63	68	64	66	64
Press – advertising/features	49	47	40	46	50	51	54	47	36	44	58	58	48	46	49	49	48	48
What's on 'listings (e.g. in newspaper/website)	31	34	30	32	33	37	38	33	25	30	42	42	40	32	32	40	34	33
Website	35	33	34	41	35	25	37	30	32	32	34	41	42	30	36	35	36	27
Posters – bus/tube/elsewhere	30	31	46	41	29	16	40	23	29	30	31	26	39	32	33	26	31	29
Television – advertising/reviews/features	23	29	34	30	28	20	25	31	22	31	22	14	18	28	28	21	27	28
By post/email from theatre mailing list	25	24	22	22	25	26	31	23	10	19	31	46	41	21	26	27	24	23
Radio – advertising/reviews/features	20	24	20	20	25	23	25	24	11	21	26	26	23	21	23	22	22	23
Poster outside the theatre	19	19	31	24	18	11	23	15	21	18	22	17	25	22	19	16	18	21
Leaflets picked up in other venues (e.g. café, shop, library)	16	20	24	21	18	15	21	17	15	18	20	17	23	19	20	12	18	21
Leaflet about shows in theatre foyers	14	16	22	14	15	12	16	15	13	14	18	14	20	18	15	10	15	16
By post/email from ticket agent/website/other	13	16	17	18	16	10	18	15	8	15	15	15	19	16	15	16	16	13
I've seen it before	14	14	23	14	14	11	14	15	14	14	12	17	15	17	13	13	14	14
The 'London Theatre Guide' leaflet	13	13	19	12	13	11	13	11	19	14	12	8	12	15	11	12	13	14
Leaflet in hotel	8	8	12	9	8	5	3	9	16	10	5	2	5	9	7	8	8	8
Tourist Information Centre	6	6	10	7	7	3	3	5	14	7	4	4	5	7	6	4	6	7
Other	5	4	6	3	4	4	3	3	7	4	4	2	5	4	3	5	4	5
Leaflets	27	30	38	30	28	23	29	27	30	28	30	26	33	31	29	21	28	30
By post/email	29	31	28	31	30	31	38	30	14	26	36	50	46	28	32	33	31	28
Posters	37	37	55	47	34	21	47	28	35	35	39	31	46	38	38	34	37	36
Media	59	61	58	59	63	61	65	62	46	59	67	64	56	59	62	59	60	61

*Performance Type key: M = Musical   P = Play   O = Opera   D = Dance

NB: Entertainment type performances are not reported here due to the small base size

WEBSITES AS A SOURCE OF INFORMATION

As part of the online survey, theatregoers were asked in more detail about the websites that they use to find information about shows and theatres. It is worthwhile bearing in mind that, as they are completing the follow up survey online, this audience may be more likely to use websites to find out information about the theatre.

From a prompted list of popular websites, Ticketmaster is the most popular, with 45% of theatregoers mentioning using the site in order to find out information regarding shows/theatres. This is followed by lastminute.com (39%) and officiallondontheatre.co.uk (30%). Nineteen per cent mention seetickets and 14% whatsonstage.com.

The prominence of websites such as Ticketmaster, lastminute.com and See Tickets (which are primarily transactional sites) alongside more general news and listings sites which also sell tickets (e.g. officiallondontheatre.co.uk and whatsonstage.com) suggests a close correlation between information gathering and ticket purchase; put simply, people research a show then go on to buy tickets.

Which, if any, of the following websites have you used in the last 12 months to look for information about shows/theatres?

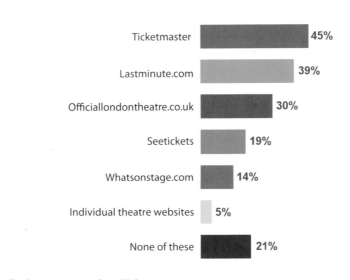

Ticketmaster	45%
Lastminute.com	39%
Officiallondontheatre.co.uk	30%
Seetickets	19%
Whatsonstage.com	14%
Individual theatre websites	5%
None of these	21%

Base: All online survey respondents (716)   Source: Ipsos MORI

Swan Lake

12 MEDIA CONSUMPTION

MEDIA CONSUMPTION

Theatregoers were asked to name which daily newspaper, Sunday newspaper, magazine, radio station and website they use/read most regularly. Although this helps build a profile of the theatregoing public's media consumption patterns, it is not fully representative as respondents were only allowed to give one name for each category. Naturally, it can be assumed that theatregoers may read/ access a number of different titles.

Nor were theatregoers obliged to record an answer for each category. Generally, there have been a number of changes in the media landscape since the previous audience survey in 2003. There is a range of new magazine titles, evening freesheets have been introduced and the internet as a source of media has increased. Factors such as this will clearly have impacted on theatregoers and be reflected in the responses we see in 2008.

As the question asked about UK newspapers, magazines, radio stations and websites, this section of the report is based on those who live in the UK – apart from the section on websites which looks at all, given the ease of accessing websites from anywhere in the world.

Billy Elliot

DAILY NEWSPAPER READERSHIP

Three quarters of UK based theatregoers (77%) read a daily newspaper regularly. This is consistent with results seen in the 2003 survey when 79% of UK residents mentioned reading a daily newspaper.

Around one in ten theatregoers regularly read quality newspaper titles such as The Times (13%), The Guardian (12%) and Daily Telegraph (9%). Smaller numbers read the Independent (2%) and the Financial Times (1%).

Of mid-market publications the Daily Mail is read regularly by 14% of theatregoers and the Daily Express by 3%.

Of the tabloid, red-top titles The Sun is read by 7%, and a further 2% regularly read the Daily Mirror.

Two per cent of theatregoers read London's Evening Standard. Of the free London daily newspapers, distributed on street and at public transport hubs the Metro, which has a nationwide presence, is read by 6%, and both London Lite and the London Paper are read by 2% each (both increase to 4% when looking at London residents only)[9].

- Male theatregoers are more likely than female theatregoers to read a daily newspaper regularly (82% and 75% respectively).

Please tell us the one, if any, UK newspaper...you use most regularly.

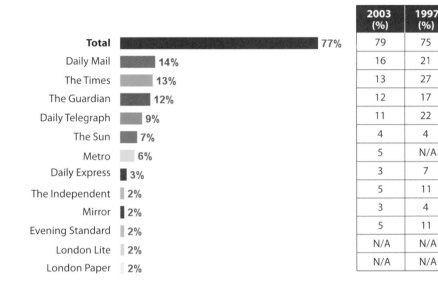

	2003 (%)	1997 (%)
Total 77%	79	75
Daily Mail 14%	16	21
The Times 13%	13	27
The Guardian 12%	12	17
Daily Telegraph 9%	11	22
The Sun 7%	4	4
Metro 6%	5	N/A
Daily Express 3%	3	7
The Independent 2%	5	11
Mirror 2%	3	4
Evening Standard 2%	5	11
London Lite 2%	N/A	N/A
London Paper 2%	N/A	N/A

Base: All UK residents answering (2008: 3076, 2003: 4081, 1997: 4964)   Source: Ipsos MORI

- Four fifths of UK theatregoers aged 55+ (84%) read a daily newspaper regularly, with this dropping to 75% of those aged 16-24 and 74% of those aged 25-34.

- Those in the older age group are more likely to read the Times (17%) and the Daily Mail (19%) than younger theatregoers.

- Conversely, younger theatregoers are more likely to read popular titles such as The Sun (12%) and free titles such as the London Paper (6%) and Metro (10%).

- Theatregoers attending an opera are the most regular newspaper readers with over eight in ten (84%) doing so regularly.

- One quarter of opera-goers read the Times (26%), a further 23% the Guardian and 13% the Daily Telegraph.

- Audience members at a musical are more likely to mention reading the Daily Mail (18%) and The Sun (10%)

- With those attending a play, the Guardian is more popular (27%) along with the Times (16%)

---

9   The London Paper and London Lite closed in 2009.

SUNDAY NEWSPAPER READERSHIP PATTERNS

Almost three in five UK theatregoers (58%) read a Sunday newspaper regularly. The Sunday Times (21%) remains the most popular Sunday newspaper amongst theatregoers, as has been the case for the last ten years (24% in 2003 and 41% in 1997 [10]).

A further one in ten read the Mail on Sunday (11%) and the Observer (8%). Popular Sunday versions of the tabloid newspapers, such as the News of the World (5%), are read by fewer theatregoers.

- Two thirds of UK theatregoers aged 35-54 and those aged 55+ (62% and 63% respectively) read a Sunday newspaper regularly.

  - This is higher than for younger theatregoers, with 48% of those aged 16-24 and 52% of 25-34 year olds reading a Sunday newspaper.

- Theatregoers of white ethnic origin are more likely to read a Sunday newspaper than those of non-white ethnic origin (59% compared to 48%).

- Two thirds of theatregoers attending an opera (62%) read a Sunday newspaper.

  - The Sunday Times (27%) and the Observer (18%) are the most popular publications amongst these audiences.

Please tell us the one, if any, Sunday paper…you use most regularly.

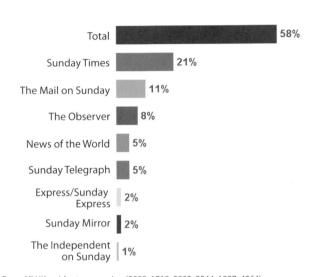

	2003 (%)	1997 (%)*
Total — 58%	64	72
Sunday Times — 21%	24	41
The Mail on Sunday — 11%	12	23
The Observer — 8%	9	13
News of the World — 5%	4	3
Sunday Telegraph — 5%	7	21
Express/Sunday Express — 2%	3	6
Sunday Mirror — 2%	2	3
The Independent on Sunday — 1%	2	11

Base: All UK residents answering (2008: 1718, 2003: 2544, 1997: 4964)
*Please note 1997 data is based on both Saturday and Sunday papers.

Source: Ipsos MORI

  - The Sunday Times (25%) and the Observer (18%) are the most mentioned by those seeing a play.

  - At musicals the Mail on Sunday (13%) and red tops such as the News of the World (7%) are more popular.

- Those earning more than £50,000 are more likely to read a Sunday paper (67%) – again the Sunday Times (34%) and the Observer (12%) are the most popular papers with these individuals.

10 In 1997 the question referred to Saturday and Sunday papers rather than just Sunday papers so this may explain the higher score.

MAGAZINE READERSHIP

Just under half of UK theatregoers (45%) read a magazine regularly. This is an increase from the 2003 questionnaire when under a third (26%) regularly read a magazine, but more in line with 1997 when just over half (54%) of UK audience members mentioned a magazine.

The range of magazine titles mentioned by theatregoers is huge and covers a vast range of topics. There are many titles that were not mentioned in 2003, and some that were popular in 2003 are no longer in the top titles, suggesting that the magazine market has been changing over time.

Due to the vast range of magazines, the number of mentions for specific titles is low. Heat magazine and OK are the individual titles to receive the highest mentions both at 3%, followed by Time Out, Hello and Grazia all at 2%. Housekeeping and DIY magazines are also mentioned by 2% and a range of women's magazines (those without enough responses to be mentioned individually) are mentioned by 5%.

- As might be expected, given the profile of titles that do receive individual mentions, women are more likely than men to read magazines (47% compared to 41%).

- UK theatregoers aged 16-24 are also more likely to mention reading a magazine regularly (61% compared to just 37% amongst those over 55).

- London residents are more likely to mention a magazine title (49% compared to 42% for the rest of the UK).

Please tell us the one, if any, magazine…you use most regularly.

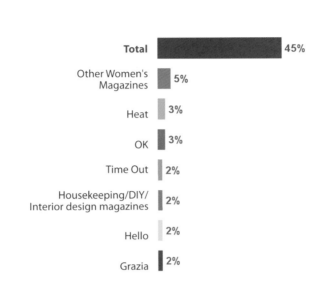

	2003 (%)	1997 (%)
Total — 45%	26	54
Other Women's Magazines — 5%	N/A	N/A
Heat — 3%	3	N/A
OK — 3%	1	N/A
Time Out — 2%	4	14
Housekeeping/DIY/ Interior design magazines — 2%	N/A	N/A
Hello — 2%	1	N/A
Grazia — 2%	N/A	N/A

Base: All UK residents answering (2008: 1325, 2003: 1018, 1997: 4964)   Source: Ipsos MORI

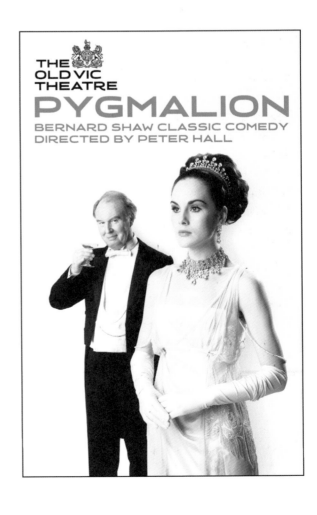

RADIO LISTENING

Seventy five per cent of UK theatregoers regularly listen to a radio station (c.f. 71% in 2003, 79% in 1997).

Radio 4 continues to be the most listened to station (19%) but has fallen a little since 2003 when it was mentioned by one in five theatregoers (21%). Radio 4 is followed by Radio 2 (13%), Radio 1 (11%), local radio stations (this covers a range of different local radio stations that have been grouped together 8%) and London's Capital FM (5%).

- Those aged 35-54 are most likely to mention listening to a radio station regularly (78% compared to 73% for those aged 16-24).

  - Radio 1 is particularly popular amongst younger theatregoers (30% amongst 16-24 year olds) and Radio 4 is more popular with those aged over 55 (34%).

- Those of white ethnic origin are more likely to listen to a radio station (76% compared to 64%).

  - UK theatregoers at an opera performance are a little more likely to mention a radio station (79%).

  - Those attending an opera are especially likely to listen to Radio 4 (45% compared to just 11% for those at a musical), as are those seeing a play (38%) and a dance performance (27%).

  - Radio 3 is also more popular with opera audiences (20% compared to 3% overall) and with those attending a dance performance (6% compared to 3% overall).

Please tell us the one, if any, radio station…you use most regularly.

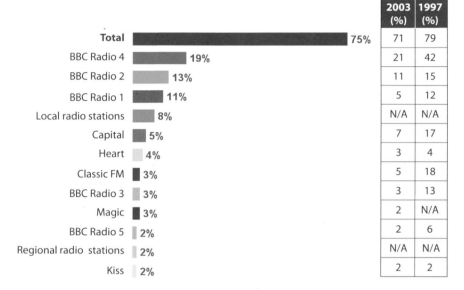

	2003 (%)	1997 (%)
Total 75%	71	79
BBC Radio 4 19%	21	42
BBC Radio 2 13%	11	15
BBC Radio 1 11%	5	12
Local radio stations 8%	N/A	N/A
Capital 5%	7	17
Heart 4%	3	4
Classic FM 3%	5	18
BBC Radio 3 3%	3	13
Magic 3%	2	N/A
BBC Radio 5 2%	2	6
Regional radio stations 2%	N/A	N/A
Kiss 2%	2	2

Base: All UK residents answering (2008: 2209, 2003: 2796, 1997: 4964)   Source: Ipsos MORI

- Classic FM is well-liked amongst those attending both opera and dance performances (9% at dance and 8% at opera mention Classic FM compared to 3% overall).

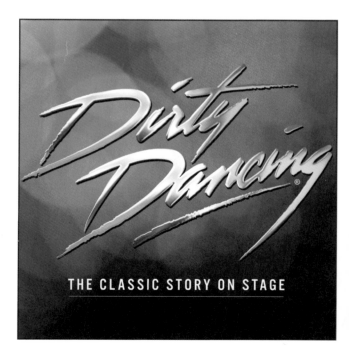

WEBSITES

Unsurprisingly given the volume of information available on the World Wide Web, the number of websites mentioned unprompted by theatregoers is large and wide ranging[11]. Just over half of audience members (52%) record a website that they use regularly. As you would expect given the growth of the internet, this has increased since 2003 when 22% mentioned a website.

Unspecific mentions of the BBC website are top with one in ten mentioning (11%). Google receives a similar level (9%), followed by Facebook (6%), Lastminute.com (3%) and BBC news specifically (3%).

- As we have seen throughout the survey, younger theatregoers are more likely to use the internet. 70% of those under 35 mention a website they use regularly compared to 34% amongst those over 55.

- Those aged 16-24 are more likely to mention Facebook (26%) reflecting the popularity of social networking amongst this age group.

- Theatregoers who are working are more likely to visit a website regularly than those who are not (55% compared to 45%), possibly reflecting a greater level of exposure to the internet i.e. use of the internet at their workplace.

- Theatregoers seeing an opera (15%) or a play (13%) are more likely to mention the BBC website; those seeing a musical are more likely to mention Google (9%) or Facebook (8%).

Please tell us the one, if any, website…you use most regularly.

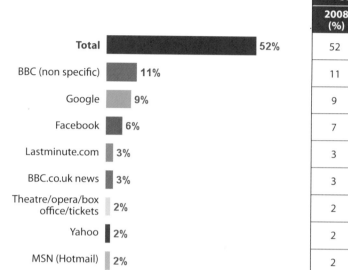

	UK Only	
	2008 (%)	2003 (%)
Total — 52%	52	22
BBC (non specific) — 11%	11	3
Google — 9%	9	6
Facebook — 6%	7	N/A
Lastminute.com — 3%	3	2
BBC.co.uk news — 3%	3	1
Theatre/opera/box office/tickets — 2%	2	N/A
Yahoo — 2%	2	3
MSN (Hotmail) — 2%	2	2

Base: Main chart: All answering 1689. Table: All UK residents answering (2008: 1539, 2003: 862)   Source: Ipsos MORI

Please tell us the one, if any, website…you use most regularly.

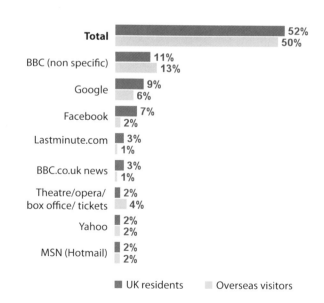

- Total: 52% / 50%
- BBC (non specific): 11% / 13%
- Google: 9% / 6%
- Facebook: 7% / 2%
- Lastminute.com: 3% / 1%
- BBC.co.uk news: 3% / 1%
- Theatre/opera/box office/ tickets: 2% / 4%
- Yahoo: 2% / 2%
- MSN (Hotmail): 2% / 2%

■ UK residents   ■ Overseas visitors

Base: All UK residents answering (3076), All Overseas visitors answering (281)   Source: Ipsos MORI

---

11 This section uses data from all who mentioned a website regardless of their place of residence.

PLEASE TELL US THE ONE, IF ANY, UK NEWSPAPER, MAGAZINE, RADIO STATION AND WEBSITE YOU USE MOST REGULARLY.

	Gender %		Age %				Origin %			*Performance Type %				Income %			Working Status %	
	M	F	16-24	25-34	35-54	55+	London	Rest of UK	Overseas	M	P	O	D	Up to £20,000	£20,001 - £50,000	£50,001+	Working	Not Working
Base	1046	1993	333	589	1025	1051	1572	1504		1433	662	692	265	962	1229	528	2294	1051
Daily newspaper	82	75	75	74	74	84	80	74		76	81	84	85	76	75	83	75	75
Sunday newspaper	61	57	48	52	62	63	58	59		58	61	62	55	55	59	67	56	53
Magazine	41	47	61	53	42	37	49	42		45	43	49	46	46	45	46	44	43
Radio station	75	75	73	73	78	76	72	78		75	75	79	75	76	76	74	72	66
Website	55	51	73	70	50	34	59	46		53	53	49	52	51	55	57	55	45

*Performance Type key:

M = Musical

P = Play

O = Opera

D = Dance

NB: Entertainment type performances are not reported here due to the small base size

13 INTERNET USAGE

INTERNET USAGE

The overwhelming majority of theatregoers who took part in the online survey use the internet at home (95%). Two in three browse the internet at work (65%) and one in five use the internet at a friend or family member's home (21%). A similar proportion use a mobile device to access the internet (19%). One in ten theatregoers completing the online survey access the internet at either a place of study (11%) or an internet café (11%).

- Use of the internet at home is fairly consistent across different groups of theatregoers.

- Those aged under 55 are most likely to use the internet at work (74% of those aged 16-34 and 78% of those aged 35-54, however these two age groups are also more likely to be working).

- Those who earn more are also more likely to use the internet at work (73% of those earning £20,001- £50,000 and 85% of those earning more than £50,000).

- Younger theatregoers taking part in the online survey (16-34) are more likely to use the internet at a friend or family member's house (39%) as are those who are members of a social networking site.

- Women are also more likely than men to use the internet at a friend or family member's house (24%), whereas men are more likely than women to access the internet via a mobile device (24%).

At which of the following places do you use the internet? And where do you use the internet most often?

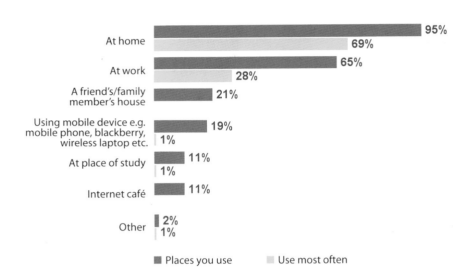

Base: All online survey respondents (716)

Source: Ipsos MORI

- Younger (16-34) theatregoers in the online survey are more likely to use a mobile device to access the internet (29%), as are those who earn more than £50,000 (31%) and those who are members of a social networking site (27%).

When asked about where they use the internet most often, home is still the most mentioned place (69%). Twenty eight per cent use the internet mostly at work with only tiny proportions mentioning use of the internet most at other locations.

- Older (55+) theatregoers are more likely to use the internet most at home (81%) whereas theatregoers in the online survey aged 16-34 are more likely to use the internet most at work (36%).

- Those earning the least are more likely to use the internet most at home (85% amongst those earning up to £20,000). In contrast those earning more are more likely to use the internet most at work (43% amongst those earning more than £50,000).

WHEN DO YOU USE THE INTERNET?

Theatregoers use the internet throughout the week, although weekday evenings are the most popular time to go online, with 78% mentioning this. The next most favourable time to spend time online is weekend evenings (59%) closely followed by weekend afternoons (58%).

This is reflected in the time that theatregoers completing the online survey record using the internet most. When asked to choose one time they use the internet the most, 41% mention weekday evenings. This is almost double the proportion mentioning weekday mornings as the time they use the internet the most (22%). This is followed by weekday afternoons which are mentioned by 16% as the time they use the internet the most.

Overall, weekday internet use dominates, 79% mention some period of a weekday as a time they use the internet most compared to just 14% for the weekend.

- Male theatregoers in the online survey are more likely to use the internet the most on weekday mornings (30%). Women are more likely than men to use the internet most on weekday evenings or weekday afternoons (44% and 19% respectively).

- Older (55+) theatregoers in the online survey are more likely to use the internet most on weekday mornings (32% compared to 22% overall).

When do you browse the internet?
When do you browse the internet most often?

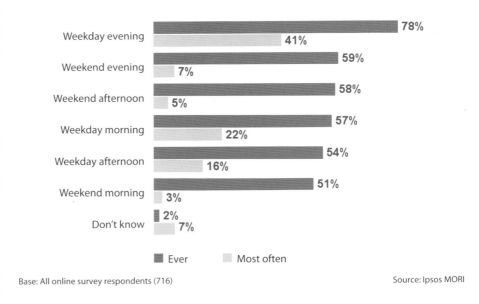

	Ever	Most often
Weekday evening	78%	41%
Weekend evening	59%	7%
Weekend afternoon	58%	5%
Weekday morning	57%	22%
Weekday afternoon	54%	16%
Weekend morning	51%	3%
Don't know	2%	7%

Base: All online survey respondents (716)

Source: Ipsos MORI

Into The Hoods. Photographer: Bill Cooper

ONLINE BEHAVIOUR

Theatregoers who took part in the online survey were asked whether they had done certain things online over the last year. The most popular activity was booking a flight or hotel which 84% of theatregoers completing the online survey have done. Almost the same proportion have bought theatre tickets online (83%) and three quarters have bought books, CDs or DVDs online (76%). A similar proportion have done their banking online in the last 12 months (72%) and have booked tickets to other events such as sports events, concerts and cinema online (71%). Three quarters also confirm that they have bought goods other than the ones mentioned online in the last year (77%).

The proportions of theatregoers in the online survey who have undertaken each of these activities is fairly consistent across different groups.

- Those aged 16-34 are more likely to bank online (82%) than other age groups, whereas those aged 35-54 are more likely to have bought books, CDs or DVDs online (82%) as well as tickets to events other than theatre (78%).

- Those earning more than £50,000 are more likely than average to have booked a flight or hotel online (93%), booked theatre tickets online (92%) and bought tickets for other events (81%).

- As would be expected those who tend to book theatre tickets online are more likely to use internet banking and make other purchases via the internet.

Which of the following have you done online over the past 12 months?

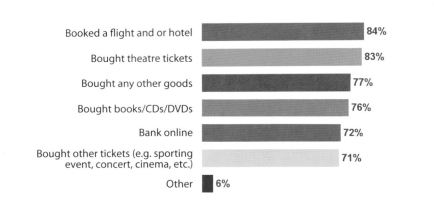

Base: All online survey respondents (716)   Source: Ipsos MORI

- Those who visit the theatre most often (6+ times in the last 12 months) are more likely to have bought theatre tickets online (90%) but also to have bought books, CDs and DVDs online (83%).

- Those who are members of a social networking site are more likely to have undertaken a number of activities – banking online (79%), buying books, CDs and DVDs online (82%) and buying other goods online (84%).

- Generally the more affluent audience is more likely to use the internet for any of the above listed purposes.

THEATRE-RELATED ONLINE ACTIVITIES

The most popular online activity related to the theatre was looking at listings of performances; this was mentioned by 87% of theatregoers completing the online survey. More than four in five (83%) have used the internet to check theatre details (location, directions etc.); comparable proportions have checked show details (times etc.) online (82%) and booked theatre tickets online (82%).

Half of theatregoers (52%) have gone online to read show reviews by journalists and a quarter (24%) have looked at reviews left by members of the public.

One in ten have read theatre blogs (10%) and purchased Theatre Tokens (9%), only a small proportion have taken part in discussions on theatre noticeboards (3%).

Which, if any, of the following theatre-related activities have you done/looked at online during the past 12 months?

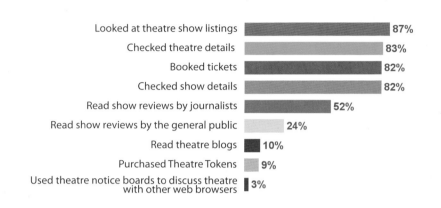

Looked at theatre show listings	87%
Checked theatre details	83%
Booked tickets	82%
Checked show details	82%
Read show reviews by journalists	52%
Read show reviews by the general public	24%
Read theatre blogs	10%
Purchased Theatre Tokens	9%
Used theatre notice boards to discuss theatre with other web browsers	3%

Base: All online survey respondents (716)   Source: Ipsos MORI

THEATRE-RELATED WEBSITES

Theatregoers were asked in more detail about the theatre-related websites that they have visited over the last 12 months.

The vast majority of theatregoers in the online survey have visited at least one theatre-related website in the last 12 months (only 9% state that they have not visited any). Ticketmaster is the most popular website, with 54% of theatregoers mentioning this site. This is followed by lastminute.com (47%) and londontheatre.co.uk (46%). More than one in four theatregoers mention officiallondontheatre.co.uk (29%) and one in five cite seetickets.com (22%).

Which, if any, of the following theatre-related websites have you visited over the past 12 months?

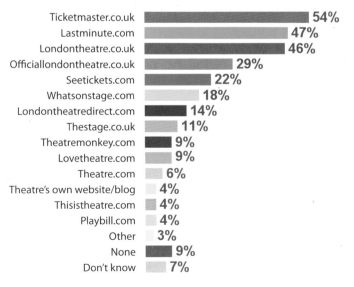

Ticketmaster.co.uk	54%
Lastminute.com	47%
Londontheatre.co.uk	46%
Officiallondontheatre.co.uk	29%
Seetickets.com	22%
Whatsonstage.com	18%
Londontheatredirect.com	14%
Thestage.co.uk	11%
Theatremonkey.com	9%
Lovetheatre.com	9%
Theatre.com	6%
Theatre's own website/blog	4%
Thisistheatre.com	4%
Playbill.com	4%
Other	3%
None	9%
Don't know	7%

Base: All online survey respondents (716)   Source: Ipsos MORI

AUCTION AND "FAN TO FAN" WEBSITES

Theatregoers in the online survey were asked about their usage of secondary ticketing sites – so called "fan to fan" or auction sites where one can buy or sell theatre tickets. Use of sites of this kind appears to be very limited – just 4% state that they have used ebay.co.uk to purchase or sell theatre tickets. The overwhelming majority have not used any of these types of websites (92%) for buying or selling theatre tickets.

- Those aged 16-34 are more likely than older theatregoers (55+) to have bought or sold theatre tickets on ebay (6%).

Theatregoers completing the online survey were asked about their attitudes towards secondary ticketing sites. As we have seen, use of these sites is limited to a small group of theatregoers and it seems that a mistrust of these sites could be influencing this.

Seven in ten (72%) agree that buying tickets from these sites is riskier than buying from official sources. Amongst this group three in ten strongly agree with the statement (32%); just 5% disagree that using these sites is more risky.

A step that might improve the reputation of sites of this kind would be launching an official industry site – more than half of theatregoers (53%) agree that an official site would provide a useful service to theatregoers and very few disagree with this statement (9%).

When looking at the situations in which theatregoers might use auction or "fan to fan" sites more than a third (37%) say that they would consider buying tickets in this way if it was the only way to purchase hard-to-get tickets (such as those that are sold out). However a similar proportion disagree with this statement (36%) and almost a fifth strongly disagree (19%).

You can now buy or sell theatre tickets from a number of auction and so-called 'fan to fan' sites. Which, if any, of the following websites have you purchased or sold theatre tickets from?

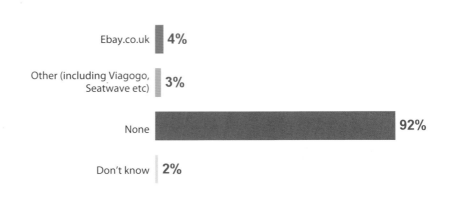

Base: All online survey respondents (716)   Source: Ipsos MORI

The following statements relate to auction/fan-to-fan sites. To what extent do you agree or disagree with each?

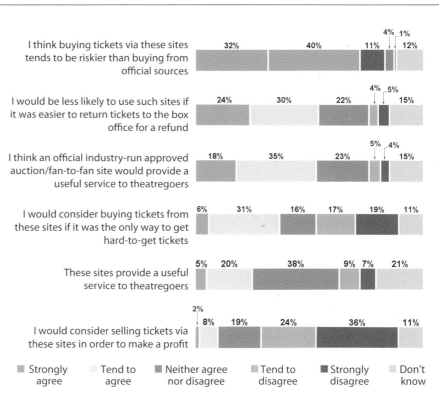

Base: All online survey respondents (716)   Source: Ipsos MORI

More than half of theatregoers taking part in the online survey agree that they would be less likely to use auction or "fan to fan" sites if it was easier to return tickets to the box office and receive a refund (54%). However a proportion of theatregoers remain neutral on this topic (22% are neutral as well as 15% who state that they do not know) so again this is not a clear-cut issue.

Only a small proportion of theatregoers would consider selling tickets on these sort of sites to make a profit (10%) and the proportion who strongly agree is even smaller at 2%. Three in five theatregoers in the online survey disagree with this approach (60%) signalling that selling tickets is not something they would consider at this stage.

Overall only a quarter of theatregoers in the online survey feel that auction and "fan to fan" sites provide a useful service to theatregoers – in fact the majority of theatregoers don't have an opinion on the provision of these services – 38% are neutral and 21% say that they don't know. This confirms the mixed picture that we have seen in regard to the presence and use of these sites.

- Younger theatregoers in the online survey (16-34) and those who read theatre blogs are more likely to agree that these kind of sites provide a useful service to theatregoers (32% and 36% respectively).

SOCIAL NETWORKING MEMBERSHIP

More than half of theatregoers completing the online survey belong to a social networking site. Two in five are members of Facebook (41%) the most popular site, while a fifth are registered with Friends Reunited (22%). One in ten are members of MySpace (11%).

However just under half (45%) are not members of any social networking site.

- Women are more likely than men to be members of Facebook (47% compared to 30%) and MySpace (13% compared to 8%).

- Younger theatregoers in the online survey (16-34) are more likely to be members of all the major social networking sites apart from Friends Reunited (which is more popular with 35-54 year olds). Seventy seven percent of 16-34 year olds are members of Facebook (compared to 14% of over 55s), 24% are members of MySpace and 9% of Bebo.

Which, if any, of the following social networking sites are you a member of?

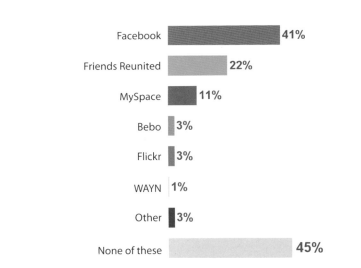

Base: All online survey respondents (716)   Source: Ipsos MORI

MEMBERSHIP OF THEATRE-RELATED GROUPS ON SOCIAL NETWORKING SITES

Among those who are members of a social networking site, a fifth have joined a theatre-related group on their social networking site.

Have you joined any theatre-related groups on your social networking site – e.g. Facebook?

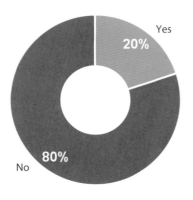

Base: All respondents who are members of social networking sites (395)

Source: Ipsos MORI

ONLINE SOCIAL NETWORK THEATRE GROUP INFLUENCE

Amongst those who are a member of a theatre-related group on their social networking site, over half say that being a member of the group does have some influence on their theatregoing (55%). It only influences one in ten a great deal, but it influences a third (34%) a little.

But for 45%, membership of a theatre-related group has no influence on their theatregoing.

Given the small numbers of theatregoers in the online survey who are members of a theatre-related group on their social networking site, these responses are fairly consistent across different groups of theatregoers.

Does being a member of an online social network theatre group influence your theatre going at all - i.e. which shows you go to see, when etc?

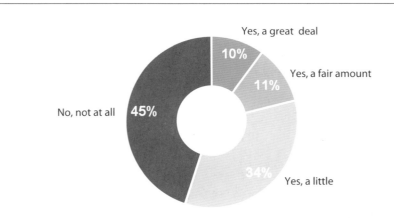

Base: All respondents members of any theatre related group on any social network site (80)

Source: Ipsos MORI

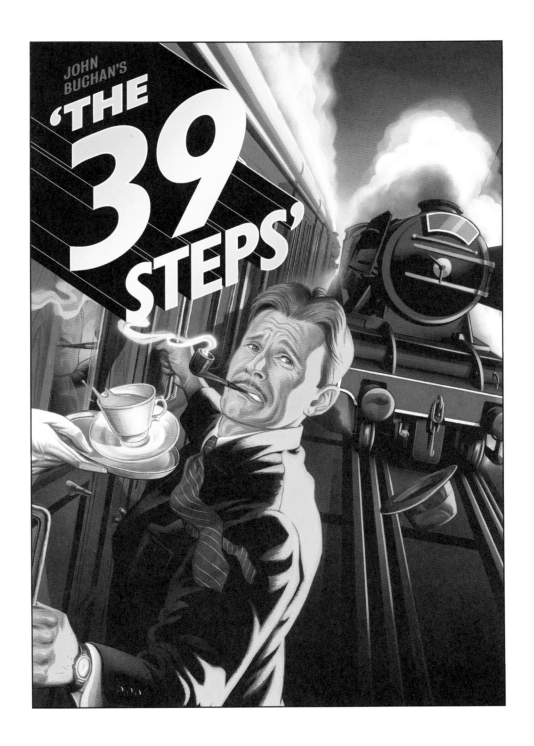

METHODOLOGY

This section of the report deals with theatregoers' expenditure associated with visiting the theatre. Theatregoers over the age of 15 were asked to record how much they have personally spent in 10 areas as a direct result of this visit to the theatre.

The 1997 version of this ongoing study used a contrasting methodology when collecting data: questionnaires were given to (and completed by) only those theatregoers who identified themselves as 'party leaders' - which meant, essentially, that they had purchased the tickets. The great disadvantage of this methodology was that it limited participation in the exercise to just a fraction of all those attending; the views of the other non-questionnaired audience members on all aspects of their trip went unrecorded.

The decision was therefore taken with the 2003 study to include all theatregoers in the research and this has resulted in much more representative findings across all areas of the report.

THE PROBLEM OF OVERESTIMATION

We do need to be aware, however, of the possibility of over-estimation or multiple-counting of expenditure now that all theatregoers are questionnaired. One can easily imagine more than one member of a party mistakenly reporting the cost, for example, of the tickets/meal/taxi fare.

We have access to a robust estimate of average ticket price paid from the Society of London Theatre, whose Box Office Data Project records actual box office receipts from all its member theatres. Using this figure we can attempt to address the problem of over-estimation and multiple-counting for the price paid for theatre tickets.

In 2008, box offices received an average of £34.89 per ticket. This figure excludes any booking fees, transaction fees, postage and packing charges etc. which might be added to the face value of the ticket. SOLT estimates that, across all transactions, charges and fees amount to c.15% of the ticket price. This takes the estimated average price paid by customers for a ticket to £40.12.

In our survey, before adjustment, the average amount reported as being spent on tickets (including those not recording spending anything) is £52.74 – this is 31.5% higher than the 'actual' average calculated from box office data and indicates that there has indeed been a degree of overestimation or multiple counting. To what extent this phenomenon of overestimation extends beyond the purchase of tickets to other areas of expenditure (food and drink, merchandising, transport costs etc.) is impossible to say with certainty. However, it is reasonable to assume that it does, and our figure of 31.5% overestimation is our best estimate to apply across other areas of expenditure.

Thus, a factor of 0.76 has been applied to all the expenditure figures reported by theatregoers in this section.

We used the same approach to account for over estimation in the 2004 data, but using a factor of 0.75 which was calculated in the same way using the recorded price of tickets and SOLT's box office data about ticket prices that year.

One result of this is that, whilst direct comparisons can be made with the data on expenditure recorded in 2003, references to the 1997 data have to be treated with caution since - as noted above - the expenditure questions were asked in a different manner in 1997 (when only 'party-leaders' were questionnaired).

AVERAGE VALUES FOR 'ONLY THOSE WHO SPEND' AND FOR 'ALL THEATREGOERS'

Expenditure results can be expressed in two ways (i) as an average calculated from the responses only of those who reported spending something; (ii) as an average calculated from all responses, including those who report having spent nothing. Both figures are useful and in most cases we report both to give the reader the full expenditure overview. However when looking at figures for different sub-groups of theatregoers (for example men, theatregoers attending a musical) we only use the average amount spent by those who do spend something.

How much money to the nearest £, will you personally spend because of this theatre visit?

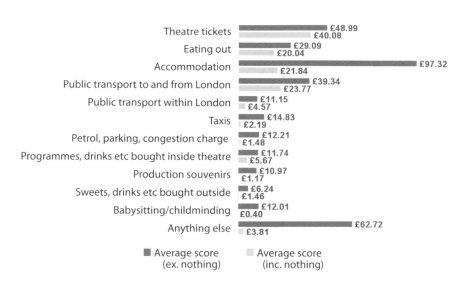

	Average score (ex. nothing)	Average score (inc. nothing)
Theatre tickets	£48.99	£40.08
Eating out	£29.09	£20.04
Accommodation	£97.32	£21.84
Public transport to and from London	£39.34	£23.77
Public transport within London	£11.15	£4.57
Taxis	£14.83	£2.19
Petrol, parking, congestion charge	£12.21	£1.48
Programmes, drinks etc bought inside theatre	£11.74	£5.67
Production souvenirs	£10.97	£1.17
Sweets, drinks etc bought outside	£6.24	£1.46
Babysitting/childminding	£12.01	£0.40
Anything else	£62.72	£3.81

Base: All answering (2008: 4586)

Source: Ipsos MORI

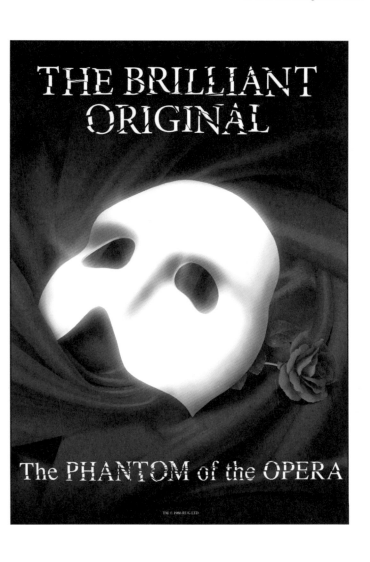

EXPENDITURE ON THEATRE TICKETS

For most theatregoers, tickets are the main expenditure associated with visiting the theatre. In 2008 those audience members who record spending anything on theatre tickets spend on average £48.99 and all theatregoers (including those who do not record spending anything) spend £40.08 on tickets.

This is a considerable increase on the amount spent in 2003 when those recording spending anything spent £36.52 on average and all theatregoers spent £31.26. SOLT's box office data shows that the average price of tickets in the West End has increased from £27.75 in 2003 to £34.89 in 2008 – this is the face value of the ticket and excludes any fees such as booking fees which audience members will have included in their reported expenditure. In 2003 fees were estimated at 12.5% of the ticket price taking the average price to £31.22. Higher fees and the introduction of other charges such as restoration levies mean that SOLT now estimates fees to be 15% of the ticket price making the average price of a ticket in 2008 £40.12.

This figure is nearly twice the average ticket price in 1997 which was £21.40. It is important to remember that this was the amount per person in 1997 rather than the amount personally spent (where an individual might have paid for the tickets for others in their group), but it is clear that theatregoers are recording substantially higher ticket prices in 2008.

- Older theatregoers spend the most on tickets; those aged over 55 spend £52.37 compared to £36.43 amongst those aged 16-24.

How much money to the nearest £, will you personally spend because of this theatre visit?

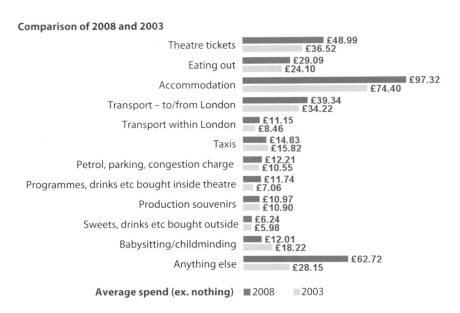

Comparison of 2008 and 2003

	2008	2003
Theatre tickets	£48.99	£36.52
Eating out	£29.09	£24.10
Accommodation	£97.32	£74.40
Transport – to/from London	£39.34	£34.22
Transport within London	£11.15	£8.46
Taxis	£14.83	£15.82
Petrol, parking, congestion charge	£12.21	£10.55
Programmes, drinks etc bought inside theatre	£11.74	£7.06
Production souvenirs	£10.97	£10.90
Sweets, drinks etc bought outside	£6.24	£5.98
Babysitting/childminding	£12.01	£18.22
Anything else	£62.72	£28.15

Average spend (ex. nothing) ■ 2008 ■ 2003

Base: All answering (2008: 4586, 2003: 6716)   Source: Ipsos MORI

- Theatregoers from the UK outside London spend more on tickets at £55.28 (compared to £40.73 for London residents).

- Theatregoers at a musical spend the most on tickets, on average £53.03, closely followed by those seeing an opera who spend on average £51.82. Those seeing a play spend the least at £37.24 . In 2003 those completing the survey at an opera spent the most on tickets, on average £69.11.

  - This contrasts with box office data, which reveals tickets to the opera to be the most expensive by a considerable way, the average price of a ticket for the opera (not including any booking fees) is £60.19 compared to £36.97 for a musical.

- As might be expected those earning the most (over £75,000) pay the most for their tickets (£65.62 compared to £41.56 for those earning up to £20,000).

- It seems likely that in some parties just one member has paid for the tickets. Those visiting the theatre in a party of 3 or 4 people spend on average £58.85 on tickets compared to £33.73 for those visiting alone.

- Those who feel their visit to the theatre was poor value-for-money are likely to have paid more for their tickets, on average £67.33, suggesting that ticket price is an important factor in assessing value-for-money.

EXPENDITURE ON EATING OUT

Two thirds (69%) of theatregoers record spending money on eating out as part of their theatre trip. This is in line with both 2003 and 1997 when respectively 66% and 69% of theatregoers spent money on eating out. Amongst those recording spending something on eating out the average amount spent is £29.09, this has increased from £24.10 in 2003, but this would be expected given inflation. Including those who do not record spending anything on eating out, the average amount spent is £20.04 in 2008, which compares to £15.96 in 2003.

- Men's average spend on eating out (£31.64) is higher than women's and the overall average, those aged 35-54 (£32.17) and those living in the UK outside London (£33.03) are also high spenders.

- Audience members who visit the theatre in a party of 3 or 4 people spend more (£34.59), potentially indicating that one member of the party is paying for the whole meal.

- Those who bought their ticket more than a month ago (£31.71) and also those who paid full price for their ticket (£32.56) spend more.

- As might be expected those earning the most have one of the highest spends - £39.84 for those earning over £50,000 and increasing to £44.08 for those earning over £75,000.

- Although the data does not identify where or what people are eating, the average amount spent indicates that many theatregoers are opting for something more substantial than a snack or take-away.

EXPENDITURE ON ACCOMMODATION

Just over one in five theatregoers spent money on accommodation in London (22%). Amongst those who mention spending anything the average amount is £97.32[12] (c.f. £74.40 in 2003). The proportion spending money on accommodation remains in line with 2003 (20%) and is higher than in 1997 when 15% of theatregoers record spending on this.

Amongst all theatregoers the average amount spent is £21.84 in 2008, (the same figure in 2003 was £14.88); the much lower level of spending here reflects the large numbers of theatregoers who do not record spending anything on accommodation.

- UK visitors spend more on accommodation than overseas visitors (£109.87 compared to £69.82 for overseas visitors). UK residents from outside London spend the most at £114.61 on average. This may reflect the type of accommodation that overseas and UK visitors choose, with some overseas visitors happy to settle for cheaper accommodation (particularly as overseas visitors tend to be younger). It could also be that overseas visitors are less likely to directly attribute the cost of their accommodation to visiting the theatre. The amount spent on accommodation also increases with age and annual income.

- Those who paid full price for their theatre ticket also paid more on average for their accommodation (£108.30) suggesting that there is a group of people who are not particularly price-driven.

- Those seeing a play spend less on average on accommodation than those seeing a musical or opera (£75.25 for those at a play, £101.59 for a musical and £113.36 for an opera).

12 A calculation was applied to the amount that overseas visitors recorded spending on accommodation as many theatregoers from overseas will have recorded the full cost of their accommodation whilst staying in London. The calculation aims to try and pin down how much of that cost can be directly attributed to their theatre visit. The calculation looked at how important a theatre trip was in the decision to visit London.

EXPENDITURE ON TRANSPORT

Amongst non-London residents (all who live in the UK outside London as well as overseas visitors) the average amount spent travelling to and from London is £39.34, again an increase from 2003 when the amount was £34.22[13]. It is important to note though that two in five of those not living in London didn't record spending anything on transport to and from London which suggests that they don't directly attribute the cost of travelling to London to visiting the theatre and this increases further amongst overseas visitors (60%). If we include this group who do not record spending anything, the average amount spent falls to £23.77; a similar pattern was seen in 2003 when all non-London residents spent on average £16.01 on travel to and from London. Those overseas visitors who did record an amount for travelling to London, spend more than double that which UK visitors spend - £69.52 for overseas visitors compared to £31.34 for UK visitors.

- The amount spent on travel to and from London increases with annual income, with those earning between £50,000 and £75,000 spending the most (£72.77).

Looking at transport within London, the average amount spent by those who do give an answer is £11.15; however, 59% of theatregoers state that they haven't spent anything on transport within London and when this group are included the average amount falls to £4.57.

In 2003, 66% of theatregoers said they spent nothing on transport within London, and the average amount amongst those who did spend anything was £8.46 and amongst all theatregoers was £2.89. In 1997, 64% of theatregoers didn't spend anything on transport within London and the amount spent per capita was £1.40.

- It is likely that the actual amount spent on transport within London is more than these results suggest: those who record nothing may well have spent something but do not directly attribute it to their theatre trip – for example, London residents may have a season ticket/oyster card and don't record any cost as this was paid for previously.

- Overseas theatregoers again spend more than domestic theatregoers on travel within London – they spend on average £16.12 compared to £9.50 for UK audience members. London residents spend the least at £6.81.

- Those earning between £50,001 and £75,000 spend the most on public transport within London, reporting an average of £20.44.

Just 15% of theatregoers record spending money on taxis – amongst those who do the average amount spent is £14.83[14]. Amongst all theatregoers the amount spent on average is £2.19.

- This amount has actually fallen since 2003 when those who spent anything on taxis spent on average £15.82. This bucks the trend of the majority of items. It is possible that this could reflect people cutting back on travel in taxis which can be seen as a luxury in the current economic situation. There has been a slight fall in the proportion of theatregoers who spend anything on taxis (17% in 2003 compared to 15% in 2008).

- Overseas audience members again spend more on taxis - £18.15 on average and those earning over £75,000 spend £18.13.

An even smaller proportion of audience members record spending on petrol, parking and the congestion charge (12%). The average amount spent by those recording an amount is £12.21 up from £10.55 in 2003. The average spent amongst all theatregoers in 2008 is £1.48, again an increase from the average for all theatregoers of £1.02 in 2003.

- Londoners spend the least on petrol, parking and the congestion charge (£6.33), this compares to £14.52 for those from elsewhere in the UK. This potentially reflects Londoners higher use of public transport. (Indeed, 88% of London residents mention taking public transport for part of their journey to the theatre compared to 76% of those from elsewhere in the UK).

---

13 A similar calculation was applied to the amount that overseas visitors record spending on transport to and from London taking into account the importance of a theatre visit in the decision to visit London.

14 It is possible that some respondents could have included the cost of taxis within both the category 'public transport within London' and 'taxis'.

EXPENDITURE INSIDE THE THEATRE

Expenditure inside the theatre can be an integral part of a visit to the theatre. Just under half of theatregoers spend money on programmes, drinks etc. inside the theatre (48%), which is very similar to 2003 (52%), but lower than the proportion spending on this in 1997 when it was seven in ten (70%).

Amongst those who spent anything on programmes, drinks etc. the average amount was £11.74, which has risen since 2003 when it was £7.06.

Amongst all audience members the average amount spent in 2008 was £5.67 which compares to £3.67 in 2003.

• Theatregoers at musicals spend the most at £13.04.

Production souvenirs and merchandise continue to appeal to some theatregoers with one in ten (11%) having spent on these items. The average amount spent by all who spent something is £10.97 reflecting the price of CDs in particular and is almost exactly the same as the amount recorded in 2003 (£10.90). If we include those who did not record spending anything the average amount spent in 2008 is £1.17 (c.f £0.97 in 2003).

• The proportion of theatregoers spending on merchandise has risen slightly since 2003 (9%) but is still not at the levels seen in 1997 (14%).

• Overseas visitors spend the most on merchandise (£18.21), particularly North American visitors (£22.28).

The Mousetrap

OTHER EXPENDITURE

For those theatregoers who choose to buy their sweets or drinks outside the theatre (23% of theatregoers) the average amount spent is £6.24, this compares to £5.98 in 2003. Including those who did not report spending anything the average amount comes to £1.46 in 2008, which compares to £1.31 in 2003.

• Overseas audience members spend more - £9.50 and particularly European theatregoers (£11.29).

• A small proportion of theatregoers (just 3%) record spending money on babysitting or childminding – amongst those who do spend on this the average amount is £12.01, if you include all theatregoers this is considerably lower at £0.40.

• This has fallen since 2003 when the average amongst those who spent anything was £18.22.

• Those in the 35-54 age group spend more on babysitting (on average £15.81) as do those earning the most (£19.97 amongst those earning more than £50,000).

The Harder They Come. Photographer: Robert Day

OVERALL EXPENDITURE

The average amount spent per person across all theatregoers in 2008 (i.e. the sum total of all theatre-related expenditure) was £118.36.

Four in ten theatregoers (37%) spend more than £100 on their visit and just 8% of audience members did not spend anything on their visit.

Looking solely at those theatregoers who have recorded an amount (i.e. excluding the 8% of non-spenders) average total spend is £128.72.

As would be expected given inflation over the 5 year period, the average amount spent has increased since 2003 when audience members spent on average £87.23 on a visit. This does appear to be a marked rise in the amount spent, with increases in the recorded costs of both theatre tickets and accommodation likely to be contributing to this.

- As we have seen, for a number of different reasons, overseas visitors spend more on average than domestic visitors - £174.07 compared to £117.72.

- Amongst overseas visitors North American visitors spend the most at £187.94.

How much money to the nearest £, will you personally spend because of this theatre visit?

Total spending across all areas

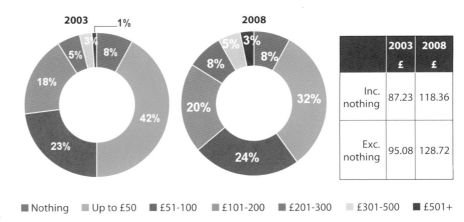

	2003 £	2008 £
Inc. nothing	87.23	118.36
Exc. nothing	95.08	128.72

■ Nothing   ■ Up to £50   ■ £51-100   ■ £101-200   ■ £201-300   ■ £301-500   ■ £501+

Base: All answering (2008: 4586, 2003: 6716)   Source: Ipsos MORI

- However, this figure for the UK as a whole masks strong differences between the average spend for London residents (£68.67) and those from elsewhere in the UK (£160.92) which is almost double that of London residents and much closer to the amount spent by overseas visitors. This likely reflects the increased costs of travelling to London and accommodation in London. Similar results were seen in 2003.

- Those aged between 35 and 54 are the highest spending age group (£149.50 on average). This contrasts with 2003 when those aged 55+ were the highest spending age group (£110.08 on average).

- Those visiting in a party of 3 or 4 people spend the most at £145.36 on average, as do audience members who booked their tickets to the theatre more than a month ago (£142.63).

- Audience members at a musical spend the most on average at £144.01 compared to £100.27 at a play.

15 TRAVEL TO THEATRE

TRAVEL TO THEATRE

Theatregoers mention travelling to the theatre by London Underground (63%) more than any other form of transport. In addition, 34% of theatregoers travel on overground trains to get to the theatre. In all, four in five theatregoers (81%) use at least one form of public transport.

One in five theatregoers (22%) walk at least part of their journey to the theatre (audience members are asked to mention all forms of transport they used so it is likely that for many people walking formed part of their journey but perhaps is combined with another mode of transport as well).

London buses and private cars were both mentioned by 16% of theatregoers. Despite work to promote cycling in London, still only 1% of audience members travel to the theatre via this mode (although perhaps performances in the evening influence this as might the relative security of cycle parking facilities).

The question was asked differently in 1997, when respondents were asked to identify only their main mode of transport to the theatre (thereby lowering results across the board relative to those in 2003 and 2008). However, London Underground and overground trains were still the most mentioned transport modes (39% and 27% respectively). Cars were mentioned by 19% of audience members, London buses by just 6%.

- Compared to 2003, the proportion of audience members travelling by tube has increased a little (63% up from 57%), as has the proportion using the overground train (34% up from 27%).

How will you travel to and from the theatre today?

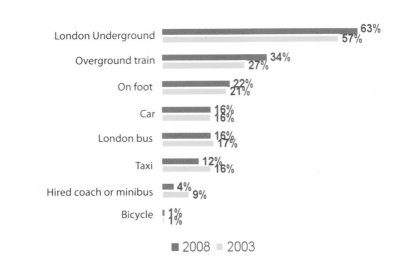

Base: All answering (2008: 4246, 2003: 6509)   Source: Ipsos MORI

- The data shows a fall in the proportion of theatregoers who travel by taxi (from 16% to 12%), whether this is because of improvements in public transport facilities, increased Black Cab fares (which rise year on year so will be higher than in 2003), or people reducing their use of taxis for other reasons such as financial pressures, we cannot tell.

- Use of public transport is highest amongst younger visitors (88% of 25-34 year olds and 87% of 16-24 year olds) and London residents (88%).

- Younger theatregoers are particularly likely to use the tube (74% of 16-24s and 71% of 25-34s), whereas those aged over 55 are more likely to travel by private car or taxi (20% and 14% respectively).

- Overseas visitors are more likely to walk to the theatre (30%). This likely reflects the fact that they are more likely to be staying centrally in London and therefore within easy walking distance of a theatre.

- Opera performances, despite attracting an older and more affluent audience, have an unusual mix of transportation – these people are more likely to travel by car (21%) but also by London bus (24%).

HOW WILL YOU TRAVEL TO AND FROM THE THEATRE TODAY?

	Gender %		Age %				Origin %			*Performance Type %				Income %			Working Status %	
	M	F	16-24	25-34	35-54	55+	London	Rest of UK	Overseas	M	P	O	D	Up to £20,000	£20,001 - £50,000	£50,001+	Working	Not Working
Base	1405	2639	530	784	1357	1315	1749	1671	747	2135	963	767	327	1246	1537	736	2734	1281
London Underground	61	64	74	71	61	52	67	58	67	64	61	59	64	63	66	57	65	60
Overground train	30	36	33	33	35	32	28	47	16	35	29	34	32	37	34	29	35	30
On foot	25	22	29	26	23	17	17	24	30	23	24	21	16	24	23	22	23	23
London bus	16	17	17	19	14	18	25	9	15	14	20	24	22	17	17	14	16	19
Car	17	17	12	11	20	20	15	23	4	16	16	21	18	15	18	17	17	16
Taxi	11	13	8	11	13	14	9	15	14	13	11	13	10	8	12	20	12	11
Hired coach or minibus	3	5	3	3	4	7	1	9	2	6	1	2	3	6	3	3	4	6
Bicycle	1	*	1	1	1	*	1	*	*	1	1	1	*	*	1	1	1	1
Motorbike	*	*	*	*	*	1	*	*	*	*	*	1	*	*	*	*	*	*
Public transport	77	82	87	88	78	74	88	76	78	80	81	82	85	82	84	73	82	79
Green travel	26	22	30	26	23	17	18	24	30	23	25	21	16	24	23	22	23	23

*Performance Type key:
M = Musical
P = Play
O = Opera
D = Dance
NB: Entertainment type performances are not reported here due to the small base size

REASONS FOR CHOOSING THEIR PARTICULAR MODE OF TRANSPORT

Online respondents (whose travel profile was, as a whole, virtually identical to that of those in the main survey) were asked some further questions about travel to the theatre.

When asked why they chose the mode of transport they did, a number of reasons were given. Convenience was the most prominent reason overall and this was the case for all modes of transport other than hired coach or minibus.

- Price is a particularly influential reason for those travelling by hired coach or minibus (59%)* and London bus (54%).

- For those travelling in a hired coach it is likely that this was part of a package with their ticket which will have influenced the price. For those using London buses price may reflect the lower prices for using London buses compared to the tube.

- Speed of travel is a key influence for those who walk at least some of the way to the theatre and amongst those who travel by taxi.

- Comfort is particularly influential among those who travel by car (40%) but also impacted on those who travel by taxi (33%) and hired coach or minibus (29%)*.

- Security is not a particularly influential factor when choosing a mode of transport but is more important to those who travel by car (10%).

- The weather impacts only marginally on most transport decisions, but rain (as one would expect) does seem to encourage some theatregoers to take a taxi (24%).

For which, if any, of the following reasons, did you choose the mode of transport that you used?							
	Total %	Overground train %	London Underground %	Car %	London Bus %	Taxi %	On foot %
Base	716	234	478	117	147	87	216
Convenience	76	76	77	71	73	75	76
Price	37	35	39	38	54	30	38
Speed	37	38	42	44	29	47	39
Comfort	15	15	11	40	10	33	13
To help the environment	10	13	9	6	16	3	13
Security	5	3	4	10	3	14	3
Weather - raining	5	6	5	7	8	24	6
For health reasons	4	2	2	5	4	7	9
Weather - nice/sunny	4	4	3	5	3	3	13
Have a travelcard/ annual travelcard	1	1	1	-	1		-
Freedom/bus pass	1	-	1	-	2	-	*
No other option	7	12	8	4	9	5	7
Other	1	2	1	2	1	1	1

Base: All online survey respondents (716) Source: Ipsos MORI

* Please note the small base size of those travelling to the theatre by hired coach or minibus. These results are indicative only.

FINDING INFORMATION ABOUT TRAVELLING TO THE THEATRE

When asked how information about travelling to the theatre is discovered, websites see the most mentions as a source of information - 44% of theatregoers mention a website of some description.

A further 41% do not use any of the information sources mentioned (it is likely that this group already knew where the theatre was). Other sources theatregoers mention are paper maps, guide books, word of mouth and ticket booking websites.

- Younger theatregoers are more likely to use websites (something that research consistently shows as younger people are more likely to have internet access and be web friendly).

- Younger theatregoers (31%) and members of social networking sites (28%) are particularly more likely to use the TfL website (again this probably reflects the younger profile of theatregoers, particularly those resident in London, who will perhaps be more familiar with the TfL website).

- Older visitors are more likely not to use any of the sources to find out about travel to the theatre (53%).

- Those earning the most are more likely to find information in guidebooks (10%), potentially reflecting overseas tourists in the audience.

Which, if any, of the following sources did you use to find out information about travelling to the theatre?

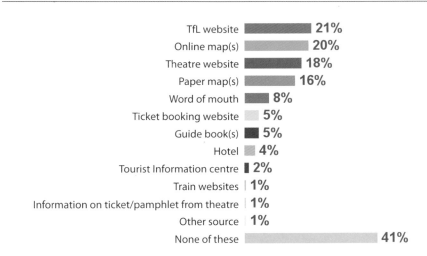

TfL website	21%
Online map(s)	20%
Theatre website	18%
Paper map(s)	16%
Word of mouth	8%
Ticket booking website	5%
Guide book(s)	5%
Hotel	4%
Tourist Information centre	2%
Train websites	1%
Information on ticket/pamphlet from theatre	1%
Other source	1%
None of these	41%

Base: All online survey respondents (716)   Source: Ipsos MORI

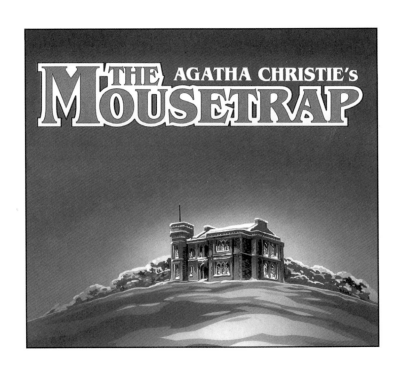

16 DISABLED ACCESS

DISABLED ACCESS

The majority of theatregoers do not record any need for special access to the theatre (83%). Handrails are the most commonly mentioned feature amongst those who do specify a need for help with access (49%). This was also the case in 2003 (54%).

As well as handrails, adapted toilets, sound amplification, wheelchair access and captioned performances are mentioned.

• Despite those in the older age group being more likely to mention certain facilities, this is not the case exclusively.

• Whilst it might be assumed that overseas visitors would have less need for specific facilities given the demands of travelling internationally, they are more likely than UK-based visitors to cite the usefulness of adapted toilets and sign language interpreted performances.

• Captioned performances are particularly mentioned amongst opera and dance audiences, probably reflecting the availability of sur- or sub-titles at many opera performances.

Which, if any, of the following access facilities do you require /find useful when you make a theatre visit?				
Facility	Total (%)	16-34 (%)	35-54 (%)	55+ (%)
Handrails	49	38	51	57
Adapted toilets	16	21	18	9
Sound amplification systems such as infra-red or induction loop	15	19	10	14
Wheelchair access	12	15	14	6
Captioned performances	11	6	8	16
Audio-described performances	6	6	8	4
Carer provision	5	4	6	4
Sign language interpreted performances	5	7	5	2
Minicom telephone booking line	3	4	4	2
More toilets	1	1	1	1
More lifts	*	1	-	*
Leg room/sufficient leg room	*	*	*	1
Other	4	3	7	2

Base: All answering (Total: 882, 16-34: 231, 35-54: 203, 55+: 416)

The Norman Conquests

WHICH, IF ANY, OF THE FOLLOWING ACCESS FACILITIES DO YOU REQUIRE/FIND USEFUL WHEN YOU MAKE A THEATRE VISIT?

	Gender %		Age %					Origin %			*Performance Type %				Income %			Working Status %	
	M	F	16-24	25-34	35-54	55+	London	Rest of UK	Overseas	M	P	O	D	Up to £20,000	£20,001 - £50,000	£50,001+	Working	Not Working
Base	292	576	120	111	203	416	355	315	187	394	131	284	56	328	289	127	468	393
Any	89	88	89	83	88	89	84	89	91	88	87	94	84	91	85	86	85	93

Base: All those answering who require some sort of facility

*Performance Type key:
M = Musical
P = Play
O = Opera
D = Dance
NB: Entertainment type performances are not reported here due to the small base size

17 APPENDICES

COMEDY THEATRE

Photographer: Carl O'Connell

METHODOLOGY

This report presents the findings of a survey conducted by Ipsos MORI for the Society of London Theatre (SOLT) during 2008. This is the fifth such survey since the inception of a programme of audience research in 1981/82.

To avoid constant repetition, this report refers throughout to the 'West End' and its audiences. In fact, these findings relate to those theatres represented in full membership of the Society of London Theatre. These include both the major commercial theatres and the larger grant-aided theatres in London.

Surveys were carried out at 37 different productions across the West End, between 12th June and 11th December 2008. The 37 performances surveyed included examples of the main types of production in London theatres: musicals, plays, opera, dance and entertainment (No shows that were classified as "performance pieces" were included). SOLT approached all of its members about taking part in the survey and those that agreed were then contacted to arrange a suitable time for the fieldwork to take place.

The relative frequency of each type of production within the project was designed to be relatively representative of a typical year in London theatre. Thus, for example, more plays were sampled than dance pieces.

Surveys were carried out throughout the 7 month duration of the project. The performances selected took place both on week days and weekends, and included a number of matinees as well as evening shows. This meant that the broadest possible range of theatregoers throughout the year in the West End was given the opportunity to participate.

The final data were then weighted in accordance with known box office data (provided by the SOLT Box Office Data Project) on audience numbers by production type. For example, 17% of survey responses were from people attending an opera. We know from box office returns that this genre actually represents 4.1% of all attendances in the West End, so the survey data were weighted to this proportion. In addition, data were weighted to the known number of ticket sales through the tkts Half Price Ticket Booth in Leicester Square, i.e. the proportion of respondents who identified the tkts booth as the source of their tickets was amended to the actual proportion of West End theatre ticket sales that the booth accounts for (2.4%).

The survey methodology replicated, as far as possible, the approach used in the five previous surveys. Each adult (15+) member of the audience was handed a self-completion questionnaire on arrival at the theatre by a team member wearing a distinctive SOLT T-shirt. (School parties were generally excluded from the survey on the basis of the age criteria.) A pen was also provided to any audience member who requested one.

The questionnaire was designed in such a way that it could, if desired, be completed after the theatre visit, folded over, and posted back to Ipsos MORI. In fact, the majority of questionnaires were returned at the theatre after the performance. This meant that many were filled in during the interval, or even before the start of the performance, as was the case in 2003; this is reflected in the fact that some of the questions relating to the performance itself generated a higher proportion of 'don't know' or blank responses than was seen in some of the earlier surveys.

To encourage participation in the survey, all those who returned a completed questionnaire were then entered into a prize draw, with a chance to win a theatre trip to either the West End or Broadway, with flights provided by American Airlines, accommodation offered by Superbreak and theatre tickets provided by SOLT.

As was the case in 1996/97, foreign language versions of the questionnaire were provided (this contrasts with 2003 when the questionnaire was not translated). The questionnaire was translated into French, German, Italian, Spanish and Japanese. These versions of the questionnaire were offered to those members of the audience where it was suspected that they did not speak English well enough to complete the survey easily. The English version of the questionnaire had the flags of all five countries printed on the front to indicate that translated versions were available.

Survey team members wearing SOLT T-shirts made themselves visible in the theatre auditoria, foyers and bars during intervals, to answer any queries, hand out pens or questionnaires to anyone who had been missed as they arrived, collect any filled-in questionnaires, and generally make audience members aware that we were hoping that they would take the time to fill in the questionnaire. The survey team were then positioned in the foyer and outside exits immediately after

La Fanciulla Del West

the performance to collect back any completed surveys.

Four weeks were allowed following the date of the performance surveyed before the returned questionnaires were collected together and sent for data-processing. Unweighted topline results of each performance were then produced and provided to SOLT and to the participating theatre. All those questionnaires which were received after the four week cut-off point were retained, and added in to the sum total following the end of fieldwork.

In total, 4,586 responses were received from the 37 different performances. This is a very robust sample size,

allowing us to be confident of the accuracy of our findings to within one percentage point. As a total of 12,693 questionnaires were handed out at the productions, this equates to a response rate of 36%. This represents a small increase on the 33% response recorded in 2003.

As well as the self-completion questionnaires, a follow up online survey was carried out in 2008. Theatregoers were asked on the main questionnaire to record their email address if they were interested in taking part in further research. Respondents were contacted by Ipsos MORI throughout the main fieldwork period. The first invitations were sent

out on 17 July 2008 and then roughly every two weeks until 12 December 2008. The online questionnaire was around 15 minutes in length. As an incentive to take part, respondents were offered the chance to win a further £200 of Theatre Tokens by completing the online survey.

The online questionnaire investigated a range of issues in more depth than was possible in the main self-completion survey – these included restoration levies, theatre based reality TV shows, internet usage and awareness of SOLT. Where possible data from the online follow up survey has been included with the results of the main self-completion survey.

SAMPLING TOLERANCES

When only a sample of a population has been interviewed, we cannot be certain that the figures obtained are exactly those we would have found had everybody been interviewed (the 'true' values). However, for any percentage given, we can estimate 'confidence levels' within which the true values are likely to fall. For example, on a question where 30% of the people in a sample of 4,586 respond with a particular answer, the chances are 95 in 100 that this result would not vary by more than one percentage point from complete coverage of the entire population using the same procedures. However, the 'actual' result (95 times out of 100) is statistically more likely to be closer to the result obtained from the survey than to be anywhere between 29% and 31%. This gives us a great deal of confidence about the accuracy of the results we have achieved in this survey.

The following table shows that sampling tolerances vary with the size of the sample and the percentages involved:

Tolerances are also involved in the comparison of results from different parts of the sample and study. In other words, a difference must be of at least a certain size to be considered statistically significant. The following is a guide to these sampling tolerances:

Differences required for significance at or near these percentages			
	10% or 90%	30% or 70%	50%
1,440 vs. 2,720 (men vs. women)	1.9	2.9	3.2
3,649 vs. 824 (UK vs. overseas)	2.3	3.5	3.8

Source: MORI

Approximate sampling tolerances applicable to percentages at or near these levels			
	10% or 90% ±	30% or 70% ±	50% ±
4,586	0.9	1.3	1.4
2,000	1.3	2.00	2.2
1,000	1.9	2.8	3.1

Source: MORI

PERFORMANCES SURVEYED

Show	Theatre	Date	Respondents
Stomp	Ambassadors	12th June	60
The Mousetrap	St Martin's	18th June	79
Billy Elliot The Musical	Victoria Palace	26th June	125
The Lion King	Lyceum	3rd July	169
The Woman in Black	Fortune	10th July	35
Into the Hoods	Novello	16th July	103
Pygmalion	Old Vic	21st July	158
Les Miserables	Queen's	24th July	105
Fat Pig	Trafalgar Studios	30th July	102
Grease	Piccadilly	7th August	155
Hairspray	Shaftesbury	12th August	173
The Harder They Come	Playhouse	14th August	30
Never Forget	Savoy	19th August	111
Blood Brothers	Phoenix	21st August	93
Under the Blue Sky	Duke of York's	26th August	71
Dirty Dancing	Aldwych	28th August	100
The Phantom of the Opera	Her Majesty's	3rd September	103
A Midsummer Night's Dream	Shakespeare's Globe	10th September	75
The 39 Steps	Criterion	16th September	68
La Fanciulla del West	Royal Opera House	22nd September	315
The Norman Conquests	Old Vic	26th September	84
Girl with a Pearl Earring	Theatre Royal Haymarket	1st October	118
Avenue Q	Noel Coward	8th October	113
Spamalot	Palace	14th October	113
Joseph	Adelphi	16th October	171
Swan Lake	Royal Opera House	20th October	170
Six Characters in Search of an Author	Gielgud	23rd October	50
Chicago	Cambridge	25th October	90
Aida	Coliseum	6th November	294
We Will Rock You	Dominion	8th November	112
Jersey Boys	Prince Edward	13th November	155
La Cage aux Folles	Playhouse	18th November	86
The Sound of Music	London Palladium	20th November	125
Boris Godunov	Coliseum	24th November	188
Carousel	Savoy	25th November	101
August: Osage County	National	3rd December	220
Sleeping Beauty	Coliseum	11th December	166

SOCIETY OF LONDON THEATRE MEMBERS

These theatres were represented in Full Membership of the Society of London Theatre in 2008. Box office data for theatre attendances in these venues, (and sales through the tkts ticket booth in Leicester Square) were used in the preparation of this report.

Where theatres have more than one auditorium, the venue in membership is the main house unless stated otherwise.

Theatres	
Adelphi	New Ambassadors
Aldwych	Noel Coward (previously Albery)
Apollo	Novello (previously Strand)
Apollo Victoria	Old Vic
Barbican Theatre	Open Air Theatre
Barbican Pit	Palace
Cambridge	Palladium
Coliseum	Peacock
Comedy	Phoenix
Criterion	Piccadilly
Dominion	Playhouse
Drury Lane	Prince Edward
Duchess	Prince of Wales
Duke of York's	Royal Court
Fortune	Royal Opera House
Garrick	Queen's
Gielgud	Sadler's Wells
Haymarket	Savoy
Her Majesty's	St Martin's
Lyceum	Shaftesbury
Lyric	Shakespeare's Globe
National – Olivier	Trafalgar Studios
National – Cottesloe	Vaudeville
National – Lyttleton	Victoria Palace
New London	Wyndham's

NOTES TO THE READER

As a guide, please note that the results for different sub-groups generally need to be more than two percentage points apart for the difference to be statistically significant, although this will depend on the size of the sub-groups and the findings themselves.

As with all self-completion surveys, the people who took part in this survey were 'self-selecting' - when the report refers to 'theatregoers', it is based on those who filled in the questionnaire. Undoubtedly, there are certain types of people who are more likely than others to take the time to take part, but it is impossible to weight the data we do receive to take account of this fact. It should also be remembered that we are not able to survey children – so the experiences and opinions of those aged 15 or younger (a sizeable minority in some performances) are not represented in this report. In effect, therefore, the results in this report are as accurate a representation of West End theatre audiences as can be achieved (cost-effectively), but there is a small degree of doubt about the extent to which they accurately reflect the views and experiences of every theatregoer.

Please note that, wherever possible (given changes in the questionnaire), trend data from previous surveys are included to provide comparisons over the last 10 years (the most recent surveys were conducted in 2003 and 1997). Where direct comparisons can be made, we have drawn these; however there are a number of points where it is hard to make such comparisons, particularly with data from 1997, as the questionnaire changed substantially between the 1997 and 2003 surveys. This means that questions either weren't asked in 1997 or phrased differently. Where 1997 data is not available in the same format as 2008, this is marked as not applicable. The 2008 questionnaire was much more similar to that from 2003 allowing us to draw direct comparisons on the majority of questions. Where there is a potential ambiguity with regard to trends we have made reference to this in the report.

When interpreting comparisons with previous studies, one important consideration is that data from the 1997 survey was weighted in a different manner to both the 2003 and 2008 surveys. In 1997, questionnaires were only given to one member of each party, rather than to every theatregoer. The data was then weighted to reflect the total number of theatregoers based on the number of people that respondents recorded in their personal party. In 2003 and 2008 questionnaires were offered to every theatregoer so it was possible for all members of a party to fill in the questionnaire. 1997 data has also been rebased to exclude 'not stated' responses - the same approach that was taken in 2003 and 2008.

There are also a number of overarching factors which may affect trends over time, e.g. the changing proportions of visitors to different types of production, or increased numbers of overseas visitors. It may also be worth considering the impact of the global financial situation as the 2008 fieldwork was conducted in the second half of that year (June – December 2008) which coincided with world-wide financial turmoil in the banking sector and beyond.

Related factors may also continue to play a role: for example, if there is a higher proportion of overseas visitors, we would expect the average number of visits to West End theatre per annum to fall, as one would not expect someone from Australia, for example, to visit the theatre in London as frequently over a twelve month period as a local resident. On the other hand, the average amount spent on travel and accommodation will rise, to take account of the time and effort involved in coming to London. We also know that people from different parts of the world can be generally more positive or negative than average when answering the same question – visitors from the USA, for example, are usually among the most positive respondents, so an increase in the proportion of Americans may well automatically lead to an overall increase in satisfaction scores.

In addition:

i) Where percentages in tables do not add up to 100%, this may be due to computer rounding, blank responses to that question, or to multiple responses to a given question

ii) An asterisk in a table denotes a value of less than 0.5% but greater than zero.

iii) Tables and charts are based on "all" unless otherwise stated.